RETHINKING
SEX

RETHINKING SEX

Social Theory and Sexuality Research

Edited by
R. W. CONNELL AND
G. W. DOWSETT

MELBOURNE UNIVERSITY PRESS
1992

First published 1992
Design by Joanna Hunt
Typeset in 11 point Baskerville
by Syarikat Seng Teik Sdn Bhd, Malaysia
Printed in Malaysia by
SRM Production Services Sdn Bhd for
Melbourne University Press, Carlton, Victoria 3053
U.S.A. and Canada: International Specialized Book Services, Inc.,
5602 N.E. Hassalo Street, Portland, Oregon 97213-3640
United Kingdom and Europe: University College London Press
Gower Street, London WC1E 6BT, UK

This book is copyright. Apart from any fair dealing for the
purposes of private study, research, criticism or review, as
permitted under the Copyright Act, no part may be reproduced
by any process without written permission. Enquiries should
be made to the publisher.

© Melbourne University Press 1992

National Library of Australia Cataloguing-in-Publication entry

Rethinking sex: social theory and sexuality research.
Bibliography.
Includes index.
ISBN 0 522 84487 1.
1. Sex—Social aspects—Australia. 2. Social sciences—Research—
Australia. I. Connell, R. W. (Robert William), 1944– . II.
Dowsett, G. W.

306.70994

CONTENTS

	Notes on Contributors	vii
	Acknowledgements	x
	Introduction *R. W. Connell and G. W. Dowsett*	1
1	Frameworks and Questions in Australian Sexuality Research *Judith A. Allen*	5
2	AIDS and the Discourses of Sexuality *Dennis Altman*	32
3	'The Unclean Motion of the Generative Parts': Frameworks in Western Thought on Sexuality *R. W. Connell and G. W. Dowsett*	49
4	Absolute Sex? Unpacking the Sexuality/Gender Relationship *Rosemary Pringle*	76
5	Sexuality and the State in Time of Epidemic *J. A. Ballard*	102

Contents

6 The 'Present Moment' in Sexual Politics 117
Jill Julius Matthews

7 Human Sexuality in Australia: The Quest for Information 131
John S. Western

References 144

Index 168

NOTES ON CONTRIBUTORS

Judith Allen is Professor of Women's Studies at Griffith University, Brisbane, and Director of the Australian Institute of Women's Research and Policy. She is author of *Sex and Secrets: Crimes Involving Australian Women Since 1880* (Oxford University Press 1991) and *Rose Scott: Vision and Revision in Australian Feminism 1880–1925* (Oxford University Press, forthcoming), as well as numerous articles in the areas of feminist theory, criminology and women's history.

Dennis Altman is Reader in Politics at La Trobe University, Melbourne, and author of six books. He has been involved in the gay movement since its beginning in Australia, and is currently a member of the Australian National Council on AIDS, the executive of the AIDS Society for Asia and the Pacific, and the Global AIDS Policy Coalition. His books include *Paper Ambassadors* (Angus and Robertson 1991), *AIDS and the New Puritanism* (Pluto 1986), *The Homosexualization of America* (St. Martins 1982), *Coming Out in the Seventies* (Wild and Woolley 1979) and *Homosexual: Oppression and Liberation* (Angus and Robertson 1972).

John Ballard, Senior Lecturer in Political Science at the Australian National University, Canberra, has been following the Australian response to HIV/AIDS since 1985 and is currently completing a book on the subject. He has also served as a member of various Commonwealth HIV advisory bodies. His earlier work concerned the impact of the colonial state in West Africa and Papua New Guinea. For 1993, he and Jill Matthews are organizing the program of the ANU's Humanities Research Centre on sexualities and culture, and they are starting research on the history of sexualities in Australia since the 1890s.

Bob Connell is 1991–92 Professor of Australian Studies at Harvard University. Since 1976 he has been foundation Professor of Sociology at Macquarie University, Sydney. He is author or co-author of eleven books and over sixty research papers. His books include: *Ruling Class, Ruling Culture* (Cambridge University Press 1977), *Class Structure in Australian History* (Longman Cheshire 1980), *Making the Difference* (Allen and Unwin 1982), *Which Way is Up?* (Allen and Unwin 1983), *Teachers' Work* (Allen and Unwin 1985), *Gender and Power* (Allen and Unwin 1987), *Staking a Claim* (Allen and Unwin 1989) and *Running Twice as Hard* (forthcoming). His current work concerns changes in masculinity, theories of sexuality, and the foundations of social theory.

Gary Dowsett is Research Fellow in Sociology in the School of Behavioural Sciences at Macquarie University, Sydney. He has worked in social research for a number of years on issues such as class and gender inequality in education, audience formation in the Arts, migrant English-language education, and since 1986 has worked full-time on HIV/AIDS research. He is co-author of *Making the Difference: Schools, Families and Social Division* (Allen and Unwin 1982), and has written on homosexuality, gay liberation, masculinity research, education, and HIV/AIDS issues. He currently works as Assistant Head of the AIDS Research Unit at Macquarie University, part of the National Centre for HIV Social Research, and is a former Vice-President of the AIDS Council of New South Wales.

Jill Julius Matthews was born and educated in Adelaide, South Australia, and has been active in both Women's Liberation and Gay Liberation since the early 1970s. She has written extensively on the history of women and of femininity. She is currently Senior Lecturer and Convener of the Women's Studies Program in the Faculties at the Australian National University, Canberra. Her book, *Good and Mad Women. The Historical Construction of Femininity in Twentieth Century Australia* (Allen and Unwin) was published in 1984, and she is currently completing *Melting Moments. Moments of Women's Pleasure in the 1920s and 1930s.*

Rosemary Pringle is Associate Professor in the School of Behavioural Sciences at Macquarie University, Sydney, and teaches sociology and women's studies. She is the author of *Secretaries Talk: Sexuality, Power and Work* (Allen and Unwin 1988), and co-author of *Gender at Work* (Allen and Unwin 1983). Her current research is about gender and medicine, notions of 'medical masquerade', and the contradictory locations of women doctors who, she feels, have been given an unnecessarily hard time by many feminists.

John Western is Professor of Sociology at the University of Queensland, Brisbane. His undergraduate and master's degrees were in psychology from the University of Melbourne, while his PhD was in sociology from Columbia University, New York. His research interests are in many areas of higher education and the professions, class and stratification and, more recently, the study of human sexuality. He is presently involved with Dr Jake Najman in a project concerned with safe sex practices among workers in the sex industry, funded by a Commonwealth AIDS Research Grant.

ACKNOWLEDGEMENTS

This book grew from the contributions of presenters of papers at a seminar on sexuality organized by the Academy of the Social Sciences in Australia in May 1990, funded by the Commonwealth AIDS Research Grants Committee. We are grateful to all those participants in the seminar, for lively discussion and continuing interest in the issues; to the officers of the Academy (Peter Karmel and Bruce Miller especially) for their initiative and practical support, and to Wendy Pascoe and Peg Job for their assistance with the seminar's organisation; and to Marie O'Brien, Yvonne Roberts and David McMaster from the School of Behavioural Sciences, Macquarie University, and Janice Mitchell, Griffith University, for assistance with various stages of the production of the book. We also thank Robert Peters for permission to reproduce his poem 'The First Kiss' from *The Male Muse* (1973) and Constable Publishers for permission to quote from Waddell (ed.): *Medieval Latin Lyrics* (1929). Finally, our thanks to Pam Benton and Graeme Skinner for endless support and encouragement.

Bob Connell and Gary Dowsett

INTRODUCTION

The human immunodeficiency virus (HIV) epidemic (and AIDS, a consequence for many infected with the virus), creating a sudden need for information about sexual practices, caught Australian social science unaware. Considerable funding became available for research on homosexual men, and some for research on other groups; a good deal has been done in the last six years or so. But this response was improvised. Most of it, like most hastily-designed research on other topics, simply applied familiar research paradigms. In an area strongly influenced by the culture of medical research, the dominant frame of mind was positivist, the main research activity the counting of what could be taken to be quantifiable facts. Some of these facts—group-specific rates of infection, rates of unsafe practice, etc.—entered policy discourses about the HIV epidemic as unchallenged conclusions, providing the backdrop for public decision making.

But as time went on, it became clear that the application of existing paradigms was not enough. More basic, and more difficult, questions about sexuality itself needed to be explored. For at the same time as a body of applied research was building up around HIV/AIDS, intellectual currents of other kinds around the world were reshaping ideas about sexuality. Indeed, conventional ideas about both sexuality and sex research have been under more or less continuous challenge for the last two decades.

The new feminism and gay liberation both questioned, from different angles, the idea that human 'sexual behaviour' (Kinsey's term) or 'human sexual response' (Masters and Johnson's) could be treated as natural facts and studied from a distance by an impartial science. The scientific gaze *could not* be neutral because sexuality is inherently a domain of power relations (between women and men, between heterosexual and homosexual, between races . . .), inherently a political arena.

This converged with the mounting evidence from anthropology of massive cross-cultural variation in 'normal' sexual practice. What middle-class white Westerners get up to is by no means the sexual standard for humanity as a whole. This further converged with an approach in sociology and social psychology that saw sexual conduct as the product of 'social scripts', learned 'roles', or 'identities' acquired through social conditioning. On this account, sexual practice seemed more malleable, more voluntary, that it seemed before.

But where, in this more social and more nuanced account of sexuality, was the source of the passion, the compulsion, the emotional depth and conflict that seems so much a part of our own experience of sexuality? As this problem surfaced, European post-structuralism and post-modernism was calling in question both the discourse of 'liberation' and the enterprise of 'sexual science' itself. As attention shifted to the discourses in which our understandings of sexuality are constructed, the notion of 'sexual identity' began to seem as fragile as the notion of biological norms of sexuality already was. In one of the terrible ironies of the HIV/AIDS crisis, a serious challenge to the notion of gay identity, a critique of the concept of 'the homosexual' as a tool of social control, was launched just before the syndrome was identified and a collective response from gay men became a matter of life and death.

These developments affected Australian researchers, policy makers and activists in the 1980s. Though Australian intellectuals have been active contributors to these debates, we cannot dodge the fact that Australian thinking by and large responds to developments in the metropoles, the

Introduction

United States and Western Europe. Witness the emergence of an international 'gay culture' and its associated style of minority pressure-group politics; witness the impact of French theory from structuralism to post-modernism. Some of this does not sit at all well with the specifics of politics and intellectual work in this country, and results in little sects rather than broadly relevant work. The effect has been to unsettle Australian thinking about sexuality rather than to move it firmly in a particular direction.

At the same time, there has been an active local politics of sexuality, centred on the state. Anti-discrimination legislation and equal opportunity policy, though not strong, is nevertheless accepted almost nationally. There have been law reforms acknowledging rape in marriage, and some degree of homosexual law reform in every jurisdiction except Tasmania at the time of writing. Compared with the situation in the metropoles, there has been a good public and policy response to HIV/AIDS, with gay communities gaining a legitimate presence in national policy making and program delivery. There has also been a neo-conservative backlash, most noticeably in New South Wales, bringing women's abortion rights in question and reinforcing homophobia. The recent murders of gay men in inner-Sydney suburbs suggest the depths that this can reach.

So reflection on sexual practice, sexual politics, and sex research in this country is timely. An opportunity for reflection was provided by an initiative of the Academy of the Social Sciences in Australia, following a seminar on the HIV/AIDS situation. The editors were invited to convene a seminar on questions of sexuality, and this book is its eventual product. The seminar was funded by the Commonwealth AIDS Research Grants Committee. We invited as participants not only people directly involved in HIV/AIDS research and research policy making, but much more broadly, people active in the various enterprises which have been reshaping ideas about the social dimensions of sexuality in general.

Our aim was to help develop an Australian perspective on the intellectual, as well as the practical, problems. How different this will be from the perspectives in the metropoles, only the readers can judge. But we think it likely that a differently configured sexual politics will yield intellectual perspectives that have their own place in global debates.

We also think that theoretical reflection has practical consequences. HIV/AIDS has aptly been described as an 'epidemic of signification' (Treichler 1988a) as well as an epidemic of disease. Practical responses, both personal and in public policy, are shaped by the meanings we find for such events and the ways we connect them to other parts of our understandings of the social world.

This book, then, is written by a group of researchers for a readership beyond the research community as well as within it. We hope to open up discussions that bear on urgent questions of policy and grassroots social action. And we hope to open questions about the meaning of sexuality, about purposes and conflicts in human life, that should be of concern to every thoughtful person in our culture.

1

FRAMEWORKS AND QUESTIONS IN AUSTRALIAN SEXUALITY RESEARCH

Judith A. Allen

INTRODUCTION

The advent of the HIV epidemic and AIDS has irrevocably altered Australian sexuality research. The crisis generated by the disease and its social context disclosed in its wake a state of knowledge, expertise and research unequal to the task of adequate public response. The history of sexuality research has been one of diversity and fragmentation; its scholars pursue vastly different approaches within a wide array of disparate fields of enquiry. Rarely would those constituting researchers into sexuality have collaborated, exchanged work or attended the same conferences and symposia. Indeed, key contributors to Australian sexuality research had never met prior to the HIV/AIDS crisis; and some still have not.

Partial explanation of the past of sexuality research and of aspects of its present lies in the effects of disciplinary and field boundaries, particularly those accompanying the academic organization of knowledge. As well, sexuality has not necessarily connoted a clearly defined, discrete field of scholarship, the constituency of which was self-evident and the research mission a matter of indisputable consensus. On the contrary, the elusive character of sexuality as a category of analysis is amply demonstrated by the often irreconcilable understandings of it proceeding from competing research traditions (Connell and Kippax 1990: 168).

Prior to the HIV epidemic, the diversity of work proceeded without too much exhortation to engage with 'outside' approaches and traditions.

Investigation of the sexual issues thrown open by the era of HIV/AIDS disclosed the dispersal of vital resources, knowledges and researchers that was a consequence of the fragmentary state of Australian sexuality research. No single standard approach to these issues as ordained by each of the prevailing research traditions provided answers comprehensive or nuanced enough to even meet the crisis, let alone to interrogate its full meaning (Parker and Carballo 1990). A result has been intense challenges to the organization and tempo of sexuality research, and not only in Western countries.

Australian sexuality research stands at a crucial crossroads. One possible outcome is the stronger definition of an interdisciplinary field of sexuality studies. Dialogue between sexologists and sexual liberation activists, psychiatrists and sociologists, psychologists and sex workers, legislators and political and cultural theorists of various persuasions, historians and members of both mainstream sexual communities and sexual subcultures, is a marked and productive feature of this moment. Some contend that the scene is set for a flowering of sexuality studies of a new kind—an innovative and pragmatic turn-of-the-century metamorphosis, incorporating the best of several traditions of sexuality research currently in place. Indeed, by some criteria, such a development is already with us (Coleman 1990; Abramson 1990a).

Those involved during recent decades in the establishment of interdisciplinary fields of enquiry are more aware than other scholars working only in single disciplines that the creation of such field studies is no 'natural' or straightforward matter. It is timely to draw on the experience of interdisciplinary programs and their scholars in the interests of setting the future of sexuality studies on the most constructive trajectory possible in the context ahead. To this end, the key characteristics of sexuality research must be identified, historically located and evaluated with regard to the problems and prospects they constitute for

1 Frameworks and Questions

the development of sexuality as an interdisciplinary and institutionalized field of study.

The elements that comprise the available frameworks for sexuality research bear particular scrutiny in the context of the HIV/AIDS crisis. Such elements include the definitions of sexuality and its associated categories currently in use within the different sexuality research traditions. As well, the kinds of expertise and approaches addressed to prevailing understandings of sexuality within these traditions should be appraised. Differences between them in part account for a decidedly disparate array of rationales for sexuality research, framed by research questions of uneven texture, density and ramifications.

At times, such differences in the elements comprising frameworks and questions for sexuality research are incommensurate. This poses a potentially serious obstacle to any easy metamorphosis of existing traditions into an interdisciplinary field. Competing readings of this potential obstacle and its possible solutions are important inputs to the evaluation of the prospects for sexuality studies.

If the cluster of issues concerning the frameworks and questions for sexuality research addressed in this chapter have transnational salience, the national context imparts some central particularities to the consideration of Australian sexuality research. A number of long-standing hypotheses concerning national identity and culture and the viability of comparison between Australian and other Anglophone countries confront both present Australian sexuality research and any devising of interdisciplinary sexuality studies in this country. These hypotheses and questions demand some provisional scrutiny prior to any sensible consensus as to the way forward for Australian sexuality studies.

The discussion has three sections. The first explores the problems and prospects for the development of sexuality studies through an analysis of the varying frameworks and questions deployed at present in the study of sexuality. The second section interrogates the case for and against the claim that these varying frameworks are incommensurable to the point of aborting the enterprise of interdisciplinary sexuality studies and evaluates possible solutions. The final section locates the preceding examination of the prospects for this interdisciplinary field in the context of debates as to regional specificity and Australian national identity.

SEXUALITY STUDIES

> sexuality: having the quality or state of being sexual:
> (a) the condition of having sex
> (b) the condition of having reproductive functions dictated by the union of male and female compare SEX 2 ... ['the sum of the morphological, physiological and behavioural peculiarities of living beings that subserves biparental reproduction with its concomitant genetic segregation and recombination which underlie most evolutionary change, that in its typical dichotomous occurrence is using genetically controlled and associated with special sex chromosomes, and that is typically manifested as maleness and femaleness with one or the other of these being present in most higher animals though both only occur in the same individual in many plants and some invertebrates and though no such distinction can be made in many lower forms (as some fungus, protozoan and possibly bacteria and viruses, either because males and females are replaced by mating types or because the participants in sexual reproduction are indistinguishable.']
> (c) the expression of the sex instinct: sexual activity (considered as a disruption of vital forces—Anthony West)
> (d) the condition, potential or state of readiness of the organism with regard to sexual activity (signs of excitation).

This definition of 'sexuality' from *Webster's Third New International Dictionary* (1966: 2081-2) locates a prevalent understanding of the term that is post-Kinsey and prior to the sexual revolution movement discourses that were textually manifest from the early 1970s. By contrast, the *Oxford English Dictionary* (1933: 582) offers a short, historically specified version:

> Sexuality ... 1800 ... 1. The quality of being sexual or having sex. 2. Possession of sexual powers or capability of sexual feelings 1879. 3. Recognition or pre-occupation with what is

1 Frameworks and Questions

sexual 1848. See Sexual ... [Relative to the physical intercourse between the sexes or gratification of sexual appetites 1878.]

If the category 'sexuality' became possible from the later nineteenth century, its currency is recent and limited. Historical protagonists active in political campaigns concerning sexuality, including homosexuality, paedophilia, prostitution, rape and workplace sexual harassment, abortion and contraception, did not use the term 'sexuality' in designating their concerns. Nor do those scholars producing the most physicalist or genito-anatomically oriented of research upon sexual behaviour have much use for the term 'sexuality'. 'Sex research' is the preferred term. Considerable confusion surrounds 'sexuality' as a category of scholarly enquiry, let alone as a meaningful or precise referent for everyday use. For any evaluation of the prospects for sexuality studies, then, an examination of current research inputs and their understanding of this central category is indispensable.

Applications and understandings of sexuality are as diverse as they are contested. Contributors to work upon sexuality deploy definitions and associated categories inflected by their disciplines and fields of origin. Sexologists, urologists, obstetricians, gynaecologists, paediatricians, psychiatrists, immunologists, epidemiologists and some varieties of social scientists such as criminologists and gerontologists are important among such contributors. Each presents approaches to sexuality forged in relatively interdisciplinary frameworks. Yet, for the most part, research derived from these fields of knowledge is framed by Webster's understanding of the term 'sexuality'. In the HIV/AIDS crisis of the 1980s and 1990s, just as in the venereal diseases crisis of the 1910s and 1920s, it was to these experts and their historical counterparts that Australian government, professions and community turned for guidance.

The sexuality investigated by this range of expert disciplines and fields is of the practical, known and (typically) measurable kind. Focus of attention is upon norms and alternatives in sexual practice, behaviour and subcultural groupings. Researchers chart the patterns of sexual arousal and stimulus. They measure frequency of coitus, duration of sexual encounters, age at first coitus, contraception used during intercourse, masturbation, erotic role-playing, uses of sex aids or toys, frequency of female and male orgasm, and sexual problems such as impotence, premature ejaculation, vaginismus, priapism, and erotic unresponsiveness (Rosen et al. 1988; Heiman et al. 1991). They explore sexual 'variations', the classification for alternatives to adult heterosexual genital intercourse. These include oral and anal caresses, urolangia, coprophilia, necrophilia, paedophilia, bestiality, incest, and the many erotic practices established within the repertoire of both male homosexuality and lesbianism. They are investigated through a range of methodologies (Toeller 1991; Pawlak et al. 1991; Gross 1991).

'Sex research' investigates sexuality as 'the condition of having sex' and the 'expression of sexual instincts' or drives. For many sex researchers, the modest goal of charting the practice of sexual activity in a scientific and objective manner is the full extent of the enterprise. Others further this same goal for the light that may be shed on other problems with which they are concerned. The gerontologist, for instance, investigates patterns of sexual intercourse in old age as part of their more general concern with the welfare and quality of life of the increasingly older population of Western countries (Bretschneider and McCoy 1988; Mulligan and Palguta 1991; Bergstrom-Walen and Neilsen 1990).

Other important contributors to sexuality research could not readily be described in terms of the same understandings, methodologies and research topics. Such contributors include sociologists, historians, political theorists, anthropologists and scholars of religion, literary critics, film and media theorists and practitioners, philosophers and varieties of cultural theorists and critics (Freedman and D'Emilio 1990; Bynum 1987; Neely 1989; Altman 1982 and 1986; Castiglia 1990; Brod 1990; Faderman 1991; Pateman 1988 and Grosz 1989). Few representatives of these fields

1 Frameworks and Questions

are to be found in the pages of the significant journals reporting on 'sex research', such as *Archives of Sexual Behavior* and *The Journal of Sex Research*, as well as the publications of various international institutes devoted to the study of sexuality (Abramson 1990b).

The charting of what sexual behaviour is and how it is variously patterned and exhibited in individuals and the groups to which they belong is not the principal concern of this group of scholars of sexuality. Instead, their focus broadly is upon the cultural meanings accorded to sexuality. This involves the study of the formation of sexual identities and subjectivities within human cultures, addressing thereby psychical, experiential and even spiritual dimensions of sexuality. Such scholars de-emphasize the study of the individual in favour of a focus upon collective or category-based sexual cultures and their meanings, although their work on the latter will often proceed through case studies of individuals. They insist on the cultural and therefore contingent character of sexuality. Genito-physiology is resisted as a base or grounding for an hypothesized sexuality upon which all else is a 'built' superstructure. Indeed the 'anatomical facts' of sexuality are posed as plastic and without the fixed significance or spatial location they are given in biomedical and psychosocial sex research.

For this group of contributors to sexuality research, the topics and burning questions for investigation stand in some contrast to the researchers in all three categories described above. The questions are of vast address and purchase, defying any easy classification. When and under what circumstances did the notion of sexuality emerge? How have its meanings changed? What relationships have pertained between sexualities and forms of cultural, political or economic power (Weeks 1985)? How are sex and gender differentiated and does the distinction remain useful or is it flawed by unacceptable conceptual and political costs (Gatens 1983 and 1989; Edwards 1989)? How have different sexual identities been historically and cross-culturally formed and with what effects on the organization of gender and sexual politics? How does the process of sexualization or eroticization of people, body parts, clothing, consumer durables and various forms of cultural production take place? Are all power relationships or relations of domination and subordination eroticized, with sexual pleasure (often of completely non-genital kinds) ensuring the complicity of the subordinated (Pringle 1988; Benjamin 1988)? Is sexual difference always or necessarily erotically privileged over sexual sameness or parity (Jeffreys 1990)? Can erotic ethics and codes—such as the centrality of penile penetration—be culturally changed and if so, under what circumstances should they be (see Altman in this book)? What are the relationships between the lived experiences of sexed bodies, sexed subjectivity and sexualized practices (Grosz 1987 and 1991)? What have been the most significant historical transformation in these relationships (Allen 1990b)? Do women necessarily come off 'second best' in heterosexual relations (Berg 1986)? Are men and women, in Freud's terms, 'a phase apart'? Can psychoanalytic frameworks be modified adequately to illuminate feminine subjectivity and sexual identities or are such frameworks inevitably heterosexist and phallocentric (Butler 1990b; Garner 1989; Grosz 1990a)? What are the epistemological implications of lesbian existence (Zimmerman 1991; Frye 1983; Harding 1991)?

The development of 'sexuality' from being a possible category to its having the currency of the past three decades is inseparable from politics. Whether pursued in the spirit of the dictionary definitions inflected by biomedical approaches or in the cultural, philosophical and historical studies modes, the study of sexuality is political. The history of its study is marked by moments of intense politicization. With its increased centrality in the formations of identity, subjectivity and social organization from the late nineteenth century, Western sexuality is a site of considerable conflict between competing political positions.

Some contenders in twentieth-century sexuality debates concern themselves with sexual practices, mores and patterns. Religious, evangelical and fundamentalist movements of various kinds evince long-standing concerns with issues such as marriage and divorce, the age of consent, premarital and other non-marital sexuality (including men's

1 Frameworks and Questions

use of prostitutes and pornography, male homosexuality and lesbianism), sex education, abortion, contraception and other forms of birth control (Weeks 1981b). In the past, socialist movements too campaigned around questions of illegitimacy, free love, marriage, divorce, prostitution, abortion and other birth control, sex education and sexual pleasure (Taylor 1982; Barrett 1980). At times, the stances and sexual politics concerns of socialists and those of libertarians overlapped; at others, these political positions diverged in their account of sexuality in the imagined and ideal future. Earlier feminists, with their concern to end the oppression or degradation of women and girls, displayed intense involvement in sexual politics campaigns, generally with advocacies distinct from those of other political positions (Jeffreys 1985; Allen 1988 and 1991a; Caine 1988). Biological determinists of various kinds, including social Darwinists and eugenicists, advanced still other angles on issues of sexual controversy, including evolution and sexual dimorphism, sterilization of the so-called 'unfit' and the resort of men to prostitution, homosexuality and forms of sexual promiscuity (Easlea 1981).

Among such diverse political positions, sexual liberalism and libertarianism dominate twentieth-century culture and society generally, and within sexuality research particularly (Weeks 1985). A genealogy of influences and 'fathers' contributed towards this end, including Freud, Ellis, Hirschfeld, Carpenter and Russell, through to Reich, Marcuse and the many popularising texts of the 1970s and 1980s (Brunt 1982). The twentieth-century scientific study of sexuality is heir to psychoanalytic, Marxist, liberal and biologistic intellectual influences. While one tradition of interpretation identifies the sexological focus on the enhancement of women's sexual pleasure as feminist in orientation, another powerful critical trajectory characterizes sexology, past and present, as anti-feminist (Jeffreys 1985 and 1990).

Alternatively, the mainstream sexual liberalism of our time is increasingly scrutinized in critical terms by newer, cultural politics positions of various persuasions. For postmodernist and anti-humanist critics, the prevailing representations of sexual norms in Western culture are little more than obnoxious and erroneous modernist and humanist fictions, which they exhort feminist and gay movements to resist (Sawicki 1991; Martin 1988; Yeatman 1989). The increasing disrepute of totalizing and universalist theories make commonsense claims regarding sexuality particular targets (Diamond and Quinby 1988). The postmodernist and anti-humanist critique of essentialism, as manifested within political positions such as feminism, often centres upon feminist work on issues of sexuality. Debates of considerable density and complexity rage between feminist advocates of anti-humanist post-modernism and feminist critics of these sexual politics positions on the subject of 'essentialism' (de Lauretis 1989b and 1990a; Fraser 1989; Fuss 1989: ch. 6; Grosz 1990b).

In this intellectual and cultural context, the study of sexuality is necessarily political and politicized. In any future it will continue to be so. Commentators divide and characterize the orientations of the biomedical and psychosocial researchers on the one hand, and those of the historical, political and cultural studies researchers on the other, in political and politicized terms. Sometimes this has been justifiable; but at others inaccurate. Do such divisions, both substantive and hypothesized, render the prevailing elements of sexuality research incommensurable? If so, the implications of this for sexuality studies as an interdisciplinary field should be canvassed.

INCOMMENSURABLE ENTERPRISES?

In 1987, two Australian experimental psychologists undertook a sex research experiment, resulting in an article published in the *Archives of Sexual Behavior* entitled 'Male Sexual Arousal Across Five Modes of Erotic Stimulation'. The essence of their enterprise was to measure and record penile circumference changes in twenty-four men aged between eighteen and fifty-two, with the median age at twenty-six. The researchers described this group as all heterosexuals, sexually experienced and sexually active. Typical sexual behaviours of the subjects included continuous lip kissing, petting, manual and oral stimulation of

1 Frameworks and Questions

genitals and various sexual intercourse positions. The group scored 16.71 on a 21-point sexual behaviour inventory used by the researchers. Their text implies that through such characteristics and measures, the group can be read as a representative, 'normal' sample of Australian men.

The researchers fitted the subjects' penises with a device called the A. Parkes Electronic Mercury in Silicon Strain Gauge, designed for measuring penile tumescence under laboratory conditions. From their 'base' penile circumference measurement when viewing 'non-erotic' material—ducks swimming—the subjects were measured with each of five different representations of forms of 'a normal, heterosexual coitus'. These forms were film, slides, written text, spoken text and fantasy (self-generated). Film secured the greatest tumescence measurements by a wide margin. Fantasy secured the least penile response. From these findings and without *seriously* canvassing the possible comparable tests that might be performed on the other group of sexed humans—women—the researchers ventured various treatments and policy-oriented uses that could be made of their work (Julian and Over 1988).

The contrast between this kind of approach to sexuality research and others is extreme. For sexuality researchers from other trajectories, fantasy constitutes, for instance, one of the most important zones for exploring the formation of modern sexual identities and the elaboration of sexual codes and meanings (Benjamin 1986). Its place in the generation of sexual desire and pleasure is not illuminated, much less gauged, by the somewhat literal and crude manoeuvre of measuring penile tumescence and dubbing the outcome 'arousal' (Ellis and Symons 1990). The frameworks and research questions of historical, political and cultural studies researchers would leave them dismayed at the minimal place of fantasy in those of biomedical and psychosocial researchers. Conversely, the lack of empirical demonstration or external manifestations of the direct impact of fantasy undoubtedly minimizes its significance in the context of the typical frameworks and research questions of these latter researchers. They would feel justified in a certain bemusement at the dismay of historical, political and cultural studies researchers. The former might accuse the latter of illiteracy and empiricism; and the latter might see the former as rarified, self-indulgent and scientifically unsound.

Unreconciled research frameworks produce tensions between researchers in many fields of scholarship other than that concerned with sexuality. This fact by no means bodes demise or non-viability. Some disciplines in the arts, humanities and social sciences, for instance, are battlegrounds between lively and competing standpoints, engaging creatively the issues at stake. Given the vast differences of approach entailed in interdisciplinary sexuality studies, is the engagement across difference (manifest in comparably contested fields) either possible or desirable? Putting this question to advocates of approaches with clear sexual politics orientations would no doubt elicit varying responses.

As a relevant sexual politics position in much significant sexuality research, feminism is a central contender in any evaluation of, firstly, the extent of incommensurability between the field's research traditions and, secondly, of any canvassed solutions. This centrality has several bases. In the first place, feminism is distinct among comparable modern political philosophies with which it has historically co-existed—for instance, liberalism, socialism, fascism and social democracy—by the pivotal and axiomatic place of sexuality in its discourses upon women's oppression and strategies for its termination (MacKinnon 1982). Furthermore, contemporary Western feminism criticizes the patterns, culture and character of Western knowledges as a crucial strand of its scholarly and cultural politics interventions of the past decade (Allen 1991b; Grosz 1988; Gatens 1991). Sexology and sex research form major targets of such critical feminist work (Brunt 1982; Segal 1983; Irvine 1990b). This makes feminist scholars of sexuality unlikely to enter into unscrutinized association with non-feminist scholars from research traditions bearing any trace of the much-problematized sexological past.

As well as the high stakes for feminism in both sexuality itself and the way it has been researched, feminist engagement with other sexuality researchers has further com-

1 Frameworks and Questions

plexities. Through the presence of feminist scholars, any interdisciplinary field of sexuality studies would import the many unresolved difficulties prevailing around the relationships between feminism and other political positions, including Marxism, those of gay men's movements, postmodernism, anti-humanism and the competing claims of Aboriginal, ethnic groups, so-called 'Third World' and decolonizing races, and religious movements (Allen 1990a; Frye 1983; de Lauretis 1990b; Martin 1988; Sawicki 1988; Bulbeck 1987; King 1990; Freccero 1990 and Smith 1990).

Finally, feminist sexuality scholars might well temper any evaluation of their engagement in an interdisciplinary field of sexuality studies with concern about the impact any institutionalizing and more formal constituting of such a field might have on women's studies and feminist scholarship within relevant disciplines. Put differently, significant areas of content overlap are conceivable. The history of Western knowledges gives feminists reason to fear that distinctly feminist analyses of issues such as incest, rape, prostitution, pornography, paedophilia, lesbianism, maternity, anorexia nervosa, beauty and the body, may be at risk (Ward 1984; Brownmiller 1976; McIntosh 1978; Kappeler 1987; Rich 1986; Martin 1989; Celemajer 1987; Wolf 1990; and Grosz 1991). Women's studies and feminist scholarship upon such topics might have to compete for research grants, appointments, intellectual space and policy credibility with a possibly male-dominated interdisciplinary field with diametrically opposed readings of these subjects (Baron 1990; Freund and Watson 1990). The impact of interdisciplinary sexuality studies might 'divide and rule' feminist scholars, with some working on 'the inside' with varying success in inflecting the larger framework of the field, and the rest working 'outside', marginalized and perhaps undermined by the influence and character of competing non-feminist work.

On grounds such as these, many feminist scholars whose work relates to sexuality studies would be sceptical about the desirability of the possible interdisciplinary field. They are more likely than other contenders to interpret signs of incommensurability as insuperable obstacles to interdisciplinary sexuality studies. For non-feminist sex researchers and scholars of sexuality, the obvious responses to this likelihood are fatalism, indifference or acceptance: sexuality studies can, indeed, may simply have to proceed without significant feminist input.

Feminism is the source of challenging and generative insights into sexual practices, identities and meanings in Western culture. It has been so for more than a century. Any more formally constituted interdisciplinary field of sexuality studies would needlessly impoverish its scope by proceeding without reference to feminist frameworks and research agendas. If sexuality studies proceeds as a viable field, the incommensurabilities between feminist and non-feminist approaches to topics of sexuality require careful exposition, analysis and interchange. This will be no small or token undertaking for any of its participants. Anger, pain and impasses will mark its route. Some beginnings have been made in this direction, including special issues of *The Journal of Sex Research*, addressing key aspects of the apparent incompatibility of feminist and non-feminist approaches to the field as it currently exists. As well, some useful recent monographs and anthologies examine aspects of the problem (Irvine 1990a).

The field of sexuality studies will be immeasurably the better if its formation becomes one in which feminist scholars can honorably make a sound investment. This is not to say that, if such a formation transpired, feminist input into sexuality studies would supersede women's studies and feminist scholarship within other disciplines. The mandates and rationales for these three enterprises are separable and distinct, while simultaneously they are mutually supporting. Hence, it would be disastrous to see non-feminist sexuality scholars emulating their brothers (and sisters) in other fields, in using the existence of women's studies as an excuse to ignore feminist scholarship relevant to their own research specialization—in other words, to self-deskill or promote selectively and voluntarily their own illiteracy (Allen 1986; Stacey and Thorne 1985).

With goodwill, an attempt to canvass solutions to incommensurabilities can be made at the foundation of interdisciplinary sexuality studies as a distinct field. The parties at this stage have little to lose and much to gain. At worst they can retire defeated after making the attempt and proceed onwards from an informed and literate if institutionally separate position, clear-eyed as to the limits and boundaries of feminist and non-feminist sexuality studies respectively.

Further important contenders in any evaluation of possible incommensurabilities in a proposed sexuality studies are gay liberation movements, especially as manifest in gay and lesbian studies. Scholars indebted to this perspective share much feminist criticism of some sexology and other traditions of sex research for 'heterosexism', for glorifying the so-called 'naturalism' and normalcy of adult heterosexuality and for participating directly and indirectly in the persecution of homosexual men and lesbians. They therefore have serious difficulty with the research priority given the projects like that described on penile tumescence and sexual arousal. They would object to the assumptions and exclusions involved in the methodology, identifying the claim of no homosexuals among any random group of twenty-four men to be ludicrous. The very notion that arousal is finally constituted simply by penile tumescence is as problematic to these scholars as it is to feminists, as is the conclusion minimizing the importance of fantasy.

Not all the difficulties that feminist scholars on the one hand and gay/lesbian studies scholars on the other would have with sex research traditions are comparable. Fundamentally, each has a different privileged category of address and constituency of concern, notwithstanding significant and extensive overlap. Put baldly, feminists concern themselves with the oppression of the sexed group 'women' by, and largely in the interests of, the sexed group 'men'. Gay and lesbian movements are concerned with the oppression and rights of 'gay' and 'lesbian' people, at least half of whom are 'men'. 'Women' as an a priori category of oppressed people is not central, and arguably cannot assume analytic centrality in much gay/lesbian theory, without disrupting or even undermining other key foundational claims. With a somewhat agnostic position, then, as to whether all women occupy a status of oppression *qua* all men, simply on the basis of sex, gay/lesbian studies would not have the same quarrel as feminists with biomedical and psychosocial traditions of sex research for their failure to locate women's oppression as a major theoretical inflection upon all empirical and experimental work.

Nor (with some important exceptions) have gay/lesbian studies scholars any inherent or *necessary* problem with the empirical traditions and methods of sex research. Indeed many of these scholars urge the need for much greater understanding of gay/lesbian sexual behaviour especially in the context of the HIV/AIDS crisis. Rather than offer meta-critique of the field of sexological work on epistemological and political grounds, they instead attack the field's heterosexism, with justice and considerable success. In other words, gay/lesbian scholars demand a place in this research tradition and make important inroads into recent publications and public policies.

Meanwhile, if gay/lesbian studies scholars demonstrate hesitation about feminist claims as to women's systemic oppression by men, they can be positively reserved about some feminist critiques of patterns in men's sexual practices and behaviours. Instances of this include some feminist arguments concerning prostitution, pornography, paedophilia, transvestism, transsexuality, bath houses, bars and other venues for public sex, sado-masochism and related sexual practices (King 1990; Freccero 1990; Rich 1986; Rubin 1981; Nestle 1987 and Weeks 1985). Gay/lesbian scholars welcome fuller and further documenting and analysis of these practices, their extent, character and meaning—for many reasons, not the least of which is the disruption of smug heterosexual norms. Putting into discourse the evidence of sexual diversity serves the interests of the substantially libertarian, gay/lesbian studies stance.

Therefore, scholars in this tradition range across the competing trajectories of sexuality research from the most empirically oriented biomedical experiments to the most esoteric of theoretical debates in cultural studies. With exceptions such as Shere Hite this is considerably less true of feminist scholars. The character of feminist critiques of positivist and mainstream Western disciplinary knowledges

1 Frameworks and Questions

obstructs any optimistic aspiration towards intervention and inclusion (Keller 1985).

As a contender in any evaluation of the prospects for any interdisciplinary field of sexuality studies, gay/lesbian studies scholars are set to see the enterprise as difficult but perhaps not insolvable. Any institutional establishment and recognition of sexuality studies is unlikely to erode the rationale for gay/lesbian studies. At times the broader framework of sexuality studies would provide an effective auspice for certain kinds of projects. The extent to which work in the interdisciplinary field would be likely to privilege heterosexual issues and risk heterosexism, however, would remain a disincentive for those gay/lesbian scholars with more pressing priorities than keeping the 'hets' honest. Within the larger field, such scholars might always be represented as sexual minorities, which could translate into battles over funding, research priorities and appointments. Objections to token inclusion might well ensue, with gay/lesbian studies scholars producing the kinds of critiques of 'mainstreaming' gay/lesbian studies that have been produced by jaded feminist scholars after attempts to 'mainstream' women's studies (Sheridan 1990).

Non-feminist and non-gay/lesbian studies sex researchers from the range of biomedical and psychosocial fields described above constitute a further large group of contenders in any future for sexuality studies. Arguably, the option of the development cannot be realized unless this group of sex researchers acquire a stake in its emergence. What have they to gain and to lose in such a possible future? This group of researchers may be distinctly uneasy sharing research and intellectual terrain with feminist and gay/lesbian studies scholars. Such unease can work on several fronts. Feminist and gay/lesbian scholars may appear to be politically biased in ways that are as partial as they are problematic. A century of sex research probably renders it beyond doubt in their view that the majority of the population are heterosexual and that heterosexuality in its many forms is therefore the 'normal' state. Sex research should surely reflect and address this. Not only does it mandate a primary focus on heterosexual sex research issues, but it also locates sexual identities and practices outside the heterosexuality as marginal, minority and, for some research frameworks, 'deviant'.

The prospect of constantly battling out the charge of 'heterosexism' with feminist and gay/lesbian studies scholars could appear daunting and pointless to those sex researchers perceiving such critics as unrepresentative minorities. They might be perfectly willing to cede space and resources to such minorities. The claim from feminist and gay/lesbian scholars that their distinct standpoints of themselves call into question the frameworks, categories and approaches of mainstream sex research, however, would probably be received as incomprehensible, at least in the terms in which it is currently formulated.

Moreover, the extent to which these potential minority scholars seek to problematize definitions and understandings of what sexuality actually is, and can be, might be a source of alarm or puzzlement for other sex researchers. At best, they might see grave practical difficulties in applying historical, political and cultural studies approaches to sexuality (as defined by feminist and gay/lesbian studies scholars) to practical research into sexual behaviour or the process of 'having sex' as the dictionary would have it. At worst, they might construe such approaches to defining sexuality as evacuating a place for any meaningful contribution from their own field of sex research at all. In view of all the remaining and measurable aspects of human sexual behaviour such scholars would like to see researched, they would understandably resist the redefinitions of sexuality that would in all probability be entailed in any interdisciplinary sexuality studies. Indeed, in reaction, such scholars might demand that the category remain 'straight', simple and commonsensical (Abramson 1990a, 1990b).

The onus is upon those who would widen and redefine sexuality and the possible missions for interdisciplinary sexuality studies to make a case for the new field which demonstrates a clear and useful place for those currently designated as 'sex researchers'. In view of their influence on policy, research funding and priorities and the process

1 Frameworks and Questions

of legislation and law enforcement, it is vital for feminist and gay/lesbian studies scholars that other sex researchers understand and seriously consider their work. Even if in the short term the substance and spirit of their work is rejected by these other sex researchers, this is better done in terms of engagement, familiarity and literacy than in those of ignorance, misogyny and homophobia.

An important strategy for producing the conditions for such engagement would be for feminist and gay/lesbian studies scholars to undertake constructive appraisals of the influential and representative writings of other sex researchers. This would involve the exercise of demonstrating how the integration of the categories, project rationales, theoretical assumptions, research questions, working hypotheses and methods of evidence collection, interrogation and argument deployed by feminist and gay/lesbian studies scholars, would improve or enhance the explanatory power and significance of the sex research writings in question.

Such an exercise would also allow the participants to identify exactly where and how different approaches were in disagreement. It could permit a more open-ended evaluation of the strengths and limitations of competing readings of the same data or phenomena, without unnecessary disparagement on either side. Indeed, the exercise could only be useful if undertaken with a due regard for an etiquette of constructive exchange and comparison. It is difficult to see how such a strategy could harm the prospects for sexuality studies. Whether it could produce sufficient goodwill to tackle the perceived incommensurabilities remains an unsolved question.

This assessment of the prospects for sexuality studies has stressed the indispensibility of a critical facing of the differences between the various frameworks and questions constituting the field, and a realistic evaluation of their probable impact upon it. The levelling or homogenizing of constituents which can occur in the construction of new fields is unlikely to be tolerated by its highly politicized scholars. The question is whether the field could be created in open acknowledgement of the contours of the relevant contests and what is at stake in them. Arguably, such contests are currently taking place anyway. Their protagonists however are less routinely aware of each other than may be altogether desirable. More systematic dialogue could be a productive outcome at least sometimes of their attendance at the same conferences and their contributions to the same journals and anthologies. The incommensurabilities between frameworks are currently and obviously salient. Perhaps they are not more so than those in place between inhabitants of other currently existing fields and disciplines.

QUESTIONS OF NATIONAL SPECIFICITY

Supposing the adjudication on incommensurabilities had taken place and researchers concerned with sexuality had decided that an interdisciplinary field of sexuality studies was in principle viable. Another set of adjudications would promptly face the design of Australian sexuality studies. These concern the significance accorded to the specific location of Australia—an ex-British dominion with convict origins, giving way to a thinly-populated, primarily Anglo-Celtic, settler capitalist society historically bent on the genocide of its many Aboriginal peoples. There are at least two diametrically opposed views as to the significance of the Australian national context for the formation of sexuality studies as an interdisciplinary field.

By one set of reckonings, Australia is a Western country, completely comparable with at least a dozen others. More specifically, it resembles the substantially Anglo-Celtic nations of the United Kingdom, the United States of America (though by the twenty-first century the combination of its non-Anglo-Celts will dominate), Canada and New Zealand. As such, there is no reason to believe that Australian cultural features, including patterns of sexuality, are fundamentally distinct, notwithstanding superficial particularities.

The consequence of this view for Australian sexuality research is as follows. With a small population of only approximately eighteen million (compared with 258 million in the United States), a relatively small higher education participation rate (especially at higher degree level), and almost no tradition of corporate and other private endowment of scholarly research, there is an urgent need to conserve limited research resources carefully. Dialogue with sexuality research undertaken in other countries therefore is crucial. Collaboration and co-operative comparison with the work of countries with bigger and more secure research enterprises is warranted and prudent. The avoidance of parochialism and versions of 'reinventing the wheel' by wasting precious resources upon Australian renditions of projects already undertaken in other countries is vital. Thus the last thing needed would be an Australian Kinsey report or an Australian Shere Hite survey. Instead, Australian sexuality researchers will do best by positioning themselves in an international frame as contributors to a transnational scholarly mission. In short, this amounts to a minimalist position on the relevance of national specificity.

Alternatively a maximalist position circulates certainly within Australia and, to some extent, *about* Australia abroad. By this position Australia is represented both currently and historically as a unique sexual culture. Influenced particularly by the work of 1970s writers and critics, Australia is the land of unprecedented male domination and misogyny. Its sexes are inarticulate homosocial 'ocker' brutes on the one hand and the 'doormats of the Western world' on the other. These cultural features have been attributed variously to: the influence of the large Irish population; the marked nineteenth-century white sex imbalance producing regions with more than three-quarters male inhabitants; the defensiveness and fragile identities of ex-convict and colonial men in relation to those of the mother country; and the homosocial framework provided by outback and bush primary industries and by Australian men's experience of war, all romanticized in masculine cultural production (Dixson 1976; Summers 1975; Modjeska 1981; Schaffer 1989).

This maximalist position on the relevance of Australian specificity is indebted to the distinct Australian preoccupation with the male line—with Australian masculinity. Whether in Russel Ward's *The Australian Legend*, Patrick White's inarticulate Stan in *The Tree of Man*, the many readings and re-readings of J. F. Archibald's *The Bulletin*, or the archetypes of Australian manhood offered in the plays of David Williamson, the films of Peter Weir or the performances of famous actors Bryan Brown, Jack Thompson and Paul Hogan, the difference of Australian men has become an international truism (Ward 1958; Lawson 1988; Lake 1986; Allen 1989). A uniquely degraded position for Australian women is predicted and claimed. This is often done prior to and, in the absence of, systematic cross-cultural comparison of identical indicators affecting women.

The logic of this positioning of Australian sexual cultures as distinct is to insist that Australian sexuality research must be fully indigenous in every respect. Hence, we need an Australian equivalent of the Kinsey survey. More generally, sexuality research is best charged with the mission of unravelling a complex and contradictory history and its influence on current Australian sexual configurations, identities and behaviours. Such a mission then offers a further co-ordinate to the project of locating the contributors to and points of engagement between an interdisciplinary field of sexuality studies and other fields. Australian studies scholars thereby become important contributors with their own distinct stakes in defining key categories and their Australian historical and cultural inflections.

Undoubtedly there are distinct features of post-war and contemporary Australian sexual culture that bear investigation. Why were Australian women the swiftest to adopt the oral contraceptive pill and on a larger scale than any other Western country in the early 1960s? Why has urban libertarianism been so powerful since the 1960s, especially in Sydney, manifest in spectacular protests around obscenity and pornography and in extensive and visible gay male subcultures (Sullivan, forthcoming)? Why is so much current Australian popular culture and comedy so anti-phallic and ridiculing of men and masculinity, as for instance in the top-rating television comedy 'Fast Forward'? Put differently, why is there so much overt sex antagonism in Australian culture?

Equally, however, there are fundamental features of

1 Frameworks and Questions

Australian sexual patternings and culture arguably common to most Western countries. If there are undeniable differences in how they are organized, deployed and displayed, it is important not to lose the forest for the trees. Areas of common transnational development pertaining to sexuality include the following: the emergence of a pattern of 'serial monogamy' in both heterosexual and homosexual populations, accompanied by high (though sex-differentiated) rates of infidelity and eventual divorce and other terminations of cohabitation; virtually uninterrupted and dramatic declines in completed family sizes since the 1870s, with child-bearing occupying the shortest span of women's lives in known history; between a quarter and a third of all conceptions ending in abortion; a decrease in the age of first sexual activity for both sexes and a corollary decline in virginity at marriage; a dramatic increase in female-headed single parent households; and the emergence of visible gay male and lesbian subcultures, neighbourhoods and cultural political movements (Allen 1990b; and Allen and Reekie 1991).

While local factors produce important variations, all Western countries experience extensive afflictions with sexually transmitted diseases, at times in epidemic proportions. In 1915 a third of the first Australian Imperial Force returned from Gallipoli infected with venereal diseases of which wives, fiancées and girlfriends were not informed, in a context of an international panic sometimes called the 'red plague' scare of the 1910s and 1920s (Allen 1990b). Venereal diseases continued to ravage Western societies until the mass marketing of penicillin from the later 1940s. More recently genital herpes, chlamydia, genital warts, and HIV infection generated worldwide alarm.

Furthermore, all Western countries so far studied have comparable patterns of sexually abusive behaviours, many of which are crimes at law, as well as sexual practices either stigmatized as deviant or problematic in various ways. If rates vary somewhat from country to country and regions within countries, certain probabilities remain, for example, for adult women of many nations today. Occasional or habitual violence by men towards women with whom they have a sexual relationship transpires in at least a quarter of all such relationships, and one in three by some research. Such violent assaults sometimes called 'battery' frequently take place in the couple's bedroom and may be followed by rape or related coercive sexual encounters. Comparable estimates of violence in gay male and lesbian relationships remain uncertain. Meanwhile, the odds of being raped at some time in the life cycle are better than twenty per cent for women. Men only face systemic odds of (anal) rape if incarcerated in all-male environments such as prisons, schools and colleges, or military establishments. Moreover, daughters under eighteen years of age have high odds of exposure to some form of sexual abuse within their family, generally from their father or stepfather. Researchers place these odds between one in ten and one in four. Finally, the odds of young women being sexually harassed in their first paid job are better than fifty per cent, while sexual harassment remains a significant risk for women throughout their working lives (Allen 1990b).

The range of services and activities often included in the term 'the sex industry' have been subject to considerable contention in Australia and comparable countries. Prostitution serving a clientele dominated by married men features in the sexual cultures of all nations, surrounded by varying patterns of legal regulation, police corruption, organized crime involvement, secrecy, and stigma or pathologization of prostitute and client (Sullivan 1991). A range of pornographic forms have proliferated in recent decades for a principally male readership and audience. They are subject to intense and unresolved debates about, for instance, X-rated pornographic videos and pay-TV, the impact or effects of pornographic representations upon men's sexual and violent behaviour, and the reconcilability between the availability of this pornography and United Nations resolutions upon the status, equality and dignity of women (Kappeler 1987). Finally, all countries studied contain a lobby promoting inter-generational sex, especially between men and boys, and equally vocal opponents, among them feminists (O'Carroll 1982; Schmidt 1990).

How can an adjudication be made between the minimalist

1 Frameworks and Questions

and the maximalist views of the salience of national specificity? Is a point of constructive balance between these views either possible or desirable? One option is to defer a fixed decision either way for the time being and to proceed with both Australian and comparative research on the vast array of sexuality issues about which more needs to be known. Often what is distinctly Australian can only be identified in the context of detailed comparative work. There is no need for Australian research to emulate the parochialism of those other countries which fail to identify their own context in comparison with others. Hypotheses, research questions and findings generated in an Australian context can yield significant returns when put to comparable contexts in the United States and Canada. This kind of comparative enterprise can be valuable for specifying what has been unique and what has been transnational. As well, Australian research can provide a basis for challenging long-held assumptions about sexual patternings and sexual cultures generalized from some northern hemisphere experience, not only in terms of their plausibility in the Australian case, but even in their place of origin.

The famous 'frontier theses' concerning the status of women and men's and women's relationships, originating from United States and Canadian historians and adopted by demographers, is a useful demonstration of the value of comparison. Women, a minority in an overwhelmingly masculine westward frontier in the United States and Canada, were a scarce commodity by this thesis. Valued by men, they faced an extremely favourable marriage market. Historically, this produced (so the argument goes) a 'mom'-centred and woman-respecting culture.

By contrast, Australian historians have reached opposite conclusions concerning the position of women using the same cause—their numerical scarcity on the frontier. Women on the Australian frontier married (young and nearly universally) men often considerably older than they were, producing many babies at frequent intervals, submitting to the backbreaking and relentless work that these demographic facts and nineteenth-century technology allotted them (Kingston 1986; Allen and Reekie 1991). They died young, poor and uneducated, having enjoyed but little female company and support due to isolation. They suffered violence, rape, drunkenness of husbands, and a generally dangerous social environment. They had poor access to leisure, information, or services like abortion (Allen 1990b).

Comparative research, however, reveals that North American frontiers were not in fact so very different to their Australian counterparts. The evidence has been available to North American historians for some time, but arguably the companionate and heterosexist assumptions entailed in dominant research traditions upon the frontier family have prevented its significance being fully appreciated. From the Australian experience of women and frontier history, careful scrutiny of the companionate frontier thesis can be undertaken. This early, pre-feminist thesis will not continue without serious modification by comparative research in progress (Allen and Reekie 1991).

This is one example that could be much multiplied as to the advantages of Australian and comparative sexuality research. Tension between the minimalist and the maximalist stances on national specificity will continue, but a constructive frame will be provided by the input of solid comparative research. The national is not to be ignored, but much clearer criteria are needed as to what characteristics are genuinely significant distinctions along with an account of their origin. Australian studies and sexuality studies have an agenda of engagement, at least in the short term.

CONCLUSION

The establishment of an interdisciplinary field of sexuality studies, though fraught with difficulties, is a worthwhile endeavour. Careful consideration of the different paradigms of its key contributors and the extent of reconciliation possible between them will be required. All contributors must remember that the category 'sexuality' is new, contingent and unstable in meaning. It has not only physiological but also cultural and psychical grounding. Notwithstanding anti-humanist criticisms of the contemporary privileging of sexuality in the definition of personhood and the discipline

1 Frameworks and Questions

of populations, the importance of the realm of sexuality appears secure for the present (Woodhull 1988). Its centrality is identified by a range of competing sexual politics stances and research paths.

Whether the importance of the field of sexuality studies elicits sufficient goodwill and open-mindedness of its various researchers to render the field to be finally viable remains to be seen. The examination offered above of the scope and character of differences between contenders and of the issues they would need to have satisfied in order to proceed, provides some basis to consider the possibilities. Certainly there exist varying degrees of incommensurabilities between the contending research traditions. Without pre-empting the outcomes of what will be taxing engagements and disputes, to work on differences—or, better, to work with them—in the formation of a more formally recognized field is a promising endeavour. Finally, whether Australian specificities should axiomatically define and organize sexuality studies is a matter for further research and ongoing debate.

2
AIDS AND THE DISCOURSES OF SEXUALITY

Dennis Altman

For good or for bad, HIV infection and AIDS has brought sexuality into the forefront of public discourse. As a result of the campaigns around HIV/AIDS we have seen public figures including federal and state ministers, judges, and someone as revered as Ita Buttrose, Australia's leading women journalist and at one point our best-known woman public figure, speaking in public about anal intercourse and casual sexual encounters. Governments, including conservative state governments, have funded community-based organizations to develop explicit messages for use in brothels and homosexual saunas, implicitly tolerating the large underground world of (sometimes illegal) prostitution and homosexual contacts.

Note the word tolerance: in many cases it is clear that prostitution and homosexuality are tolerated as facts of life which need be dealt with—in terms of the HIV epidemic, often because it is assumed that 'bisexual men' will spread the virus into 'the general community'—but not accepted. When the Western Australian Parliament decriminalized sodomy in 1989, partly because of the insistence by the state government that this was necessary as part of the national effort against HIV/AIDS, it also included a preamble to the relevant Act saying that: 'The Parliament disapproves of sexual relations between persons of the same sex [and] . . . does not wish to create a change in community attitudes to homosexual behaviour' (Carr 1990: 12). (However a similar preamble was not included in Queensland legislation the

2 AIDS and the Discourses of Sexuality

following year, nor in the legislation introduced by the Tasmanian Government, but to date blocked in that state's Upper House.) Many of the recommendations on prostitution made in the Federal Government's 1989 White Paper on HIV/AIDS—which was developed after an exhaustive process of national consultation and accepted in principle by all Australian governments as the basis for a national strategy for handling the epidemic—have not been acted upon (Watchirs 1991).

Nor have HIV/AIDS prevention campaigns been without controversy: there is a widespread feeling that what can be said to an audience defined as 'gay' is still unacceptable when it goes beyond these boundaries. When the Victorian AIDS Council released a poster aimed at young men who might be tempted to experiment with homosexual sex it unleashed a political storm, including a decision by the Advertising Standards Council to censor the advertisement (Goggin and Hee 1990). But unlike the United States, where conservatives in Congress have forced the ban of any educational/prevention material which could be construed as 'promoting' anything other than monogamous heterosexuality, there has been a remarkable tolerance in Australia for material directed at HIV/AIDS prevention which is both sex-positive and specifically pro-gay.

While HIV/AIDS has altered the public discourse around sexuality in general, its impact has been particularly marked on homosexuality. Given the initial construction of the disease as 'the gay plague' and the epidemiological reality that the vast majority of cases so far known in Australia have been due to homosexual contact, this is hardly surprising. What may be surprising is that on balance the HIV epidemic has probably contributed to a greater recognition and legitimacy for homosexuality in Australian society; not the outcome most would have predicted if presented with the spectre of the epidemic a decade ago.

BEHAVIOUR AND IDENTITY

If HIV/AIDS has meant a clear change in the public discourses around sexuality, it has clearly not affected behaviour to the same extent. Indeed, it is the drive to make the latter catch up with the former that has driven many of the education programs and socio-behavioural research activities which have developed in response to HIV/AIDS. Nor have the shifts in discourse been all in the same direction. Rather, they have ranged from the moral right's insistence that sexual permissiveness is inherently wicked and leads directly to punishment from God (thus AIDS becomes literally a mark of divine displeasure) through to publications produced by various community-based organizations which extol 'safe sex' as a means of expanding sexual adventure. Both gay and sex-worker organizations have run workshops aimed at expanding various forms of sexual behaviour and expanding sexual repertoires.

The threat of sexual transmission of HIV has meant a major boost for research into sexuality. Just as HIV/AIDS has raised the status of venereology in medical research, so too the threat of a worldwide pandemic has raised the respectability of sociological, psychological and anthropological research into sexuality. The Global Programme on AIDS (GPA) has sponsored a number of KAPB (Knowledge, Attitudes, Practices, Behaviour) studies on sexual behaviour, which adopted a strongly constructionist perspective on sexuality (Carballo et al. 1989). Since the appointment of Mike Merson to head the GPA in 1990, support for such research programs has declined. Even so, the greater part of sex research connected with HIV/AIDS tends to concentrate on behaviour rather than either the individual or social meanings and fantasies attached to sexuality (Turner 1989). I cheerfully admit that I find much of this research irrelevant, and some of it impenetrable, such as one study which used copious statistical analysis to develop 'the concept of worst case sexual mixing' (Kaplan 1989).

One of the crucial issues about any research related to sexuality is the different meanings which people attribute to the same terms. 'When I use a word,' said Humpty Dumpty, 'it means whatever I want it to mean.' This is very true of terms such as 'promiscuity' and 'monogamy', which often feature in discussions of what constitutes 'risky' sexual behaviour. As research currently being undertaken in Melbourne by Rosenthal et al. (1990) has stressed, mono-

2 AIDS and the Discourses of Sexuality

gamy for adolescents means serial monogamy, and the average adolescent relationship lasts for less than a year. Hence adolescents, who may feel they are at no risk of contracting HIV because they are in a 'monogamous relationship', may be making a very dangerous assumption. Similar confusion applies to the term 'prostitution': the relationship between sex and money is a culturally relativist one, and the understanding of who is a prostitute or what constitutes sex work is largely dependent on the social context.

How we understand the meanings of sexuality may be more significant than measuring actual sexual behaviour. As Watney has argued:

> Behaviourism so critically lacks any theory of *desire*, for which it substitutes a mechanically and profoundly problematic notion of 'sex', taken as an a priori reality that blinds researchers to the multiple, uneven, shifting relations of desire to sexual behaviour and identities, both in the lives of individuals and desiring collectivities. (Watney 1990: 20)

The failure of most behavioural research to fully contextualize sexual behaviour within its social, cultural and political settings means that discussion of the impact of the HIV epidemic on the gay community—as distinct from individual gay men—has been far more discussed in the gay press than in academic journals.[1] And yet the most remarkable fact about the impact of HIV/AIDS on sexuality in Western countries such as Australia has been its effect upon the self-image and the broader perception of the gay community. The whole course of the epidemic in the developed world has been fundamentally shaped by the late twentieth-century assumptions about (homo)sexual identity, assumptions which mean organizational and educational responses to HIV/AIDS which would be meaningless in societies where (homo)sexual identity was very different. One concrete example is the reluctance of many Hispanic and black organizations in the United States to recognize that homosexual behaviour exists in their communities, thus slowing down dramatically the provision of effective HIV/AIDS education material.

In a sense much of the academic literature on sexuality

takes for granted precisely what it needs throw into question, namely the creation and persistence of sexual identities. The original construction of HIV/AIDS as affecting 'risk groups' rather than 'risk behaviours' continues to inform research. There is constant reference by researchers to 'gay men' and the 'gay community', neither of which phrase accurately describes those other men who have sex with men. (Indeed, the phrase 'men who have sex with men' is increasingly being used by HIV/AIDS educators to overcome these confusions.) The basic distinction between behaviour and identity has to be constantly stressed: people are not simply 'homosexual'; rather, many people engage in homosexual acts—and many, not always the same ones, experience homosexual fantasies—which for a minority becomes a basis for a concept of homosexual (lesbian/gay) identity. As Pateman put it: 'The self is not completely subsumed in its sexuality, but identity is inseparable from the social construction of the self' (Pateman 1988, see ch. 7). The distinction between homosexual behaviour and identity, first identified in sociological literature by McIntosh at the end of the 1960s (McIntosh 1968), is the basis for the modern idea of the 'gay community' (or 'lesbian/gay community') in which an ethnic model of identity becomes the basis for social, cultural and political organization around sexual preference (Epstein 1987). This community can, of course, include people who are celibate, virgins, impotent, or even those more likely to practise heterosexual than homosexual sex. The crucial factor is how they define their public personae, and how it is perceived by others. Pronger has suggested a further way of conceptualising sexuality, seeing it as 'a way of being and understanding': 'Rather than defining a person, "homosexuality" and "heterosexuality" describe modes of being in the world, fluid ways of perceiving or interpreting oneself and others in gendered culture' (Pronger 1990: 8).

Ironically, the concepts of 'identity/community' have been taken up to describe groups that are even less coherent than men who have sex with men, so one often encounters discussion of the 'heterosexual community', a misuse of the term equivalent to that of politicians who

2 AIDS and the Discourses of Sexuality

speak of the 'community' when they mean the entire society. One of the most interesting developments spurred by HIV/AIDS is the self-conscious attempt by some to construct a 'community' of injecting drug users on the gay community model—but that goes well beyond the scope of this discussion.

The distinction between behaviour and identity is particularly important in non-Western countries, where it is assumed either that Western concepts of gayness can be applied to all manifestations of homosexuality or, alternatively, that the social/cultural differences are so great that no gay identity exists. Both of these positions are misleading. It is clear that in many Third World cities—Bangkok, Rio de Janeiro and Mexico City above all, but also in Soweto, Seoul and Santiago—there are a number of men (though fewer women) who conceive of themselves as 'gay', as we use that term, but also that they probably make up a smaller proportion of the homosexually active population than is true in, say, Sydney, Hamburg or Toronto. It is also true that there is a considerable diversity of homosexualities in all societies, and that a middle-class Thai or Costa Rican calling himself 'gay' will have a great deal in common with a 'gay man' in the Netherlands or New Zealand. In Rio de Janeiro and in Bangkok, two Third World cities renowned for their homosexual life, I have been struck by the range of gay life—from elegant saunas and clubs to street prostitution and grubby movie houses—but also by the fact that in many ways the patterns are not nearly as dissimilar from those of Western cities as one might expect. Indeed it has been argued, most notably by Whitam and Mathy (1985), that this points to a cross-cultural expression of homosexuality which is present in all societies.

It would be more accurate to point out that there often exist two very different models of homosexuality in many non-Western countries: the first being the traditional expression of sexuality between men, often according to norms and values which are quite different from the second, which is an expression of homosexuality influenced by Western forms.[2] Thus in many Middle Eastern countries, where sex between men has a long tradition often commemorated in literature and music, homosexuality is now officially proscribed and persecuted; e.g. there are frequent reports of very violent persecution of homosexuals in Iran. In a number of countries homosexuality is both defined as a Western perversion while condemned for failure to uphold values themselves derived from the West.

This has immediate implications for both policy and research in countries where there is an official position which denies the existence of homosexuality, or can only explain it as an example of 'Western decadence' (as in China, Libya or Pinochet's Chile). Taboos on discussion of homosexuality among both blacks and whites in South Africa, for example, have meant a tragic lack of appropriate interventions to prevent homosexual transmission of HIV in that country (Moodie 1989). By 1990 the African National Congress had become sufficiently aware of the toll AIDS was taking in the countries north of South Africa—many of which are major sources of labour for South Africa—to recognize the need to develop appropriate policies.

HOMOSEXUALITY: SEX AND IDENTITY

It is not accidental that Havelock Ellis, Freud and Foucault all began their discussions of sexuality with considerable reflection on homosexuality. Current support for research on the comparative construction of homosexual identities allows us to see the enormous diversity in human sexuality, indeed in what we consider to be sexual. (Martha McIntyre has pointed out to me that in some societies homosexual behaviour is defined as play rather than sex, which allows respondents to assure visiting anthropologists and officials that their society has no homosexuality.) Our society contains fair amounts of homoerotic behaviour—especially on football fields—which is never defined as sexual. One of the striking effects of the HIV epidemic is that by increasing public willingness to discuss homosexuality it also allows permission to discuss sexuality in general. This is perhaps most obvious in schools, where some states have instituted 'mandatory' HIV/AIDS education. Despite the difficulty in

2 AIDS and the Discourses of Sexuality

knowing exactly what this has meant in practice, clearly it has opened up the range of discussion of sexuality to which many school children are exposed.

A considerable amount of information about homosexual behaviour/identity now exists because of HIV-related research. The Social Aspects of Prevention of AIDS (SAPA) studies, a joint undertaking of the AIDS Council of New South Wales and Macquarie University, are charting in a way never before attempted in Australia an ethnography of gay behaviour and identity (Connell et al. 1989; Connell and Kippax 1990). These are far more sophisticated in technique and scope than most overseas research, which tends to be simply quantitative with a strong emphasis on counting numbers of partners and condom use rather than understanding the tissue of social meanings within which sexual behaviour takes place. One of the reasons for the sophistication of the Macquarie University team's research is that they come to the questions with a deep familiarity with the theoretical debates about the construction of sexuality and the considerable literature produced by the gay movement itself—which is not true of many of the researchers who have turned to this area in recent years.

There is a particular problem with any survey research into homosexual behaviour, and that is the question of the sample. As we do not know the total distribution within the population of men who have sex with men, no sample or study can be totally representative (and almost all will over-represent those men who identify with or at least make use of gay institutions). Several years ago a workshop in Sydney spent a lot of time agonising whether the SAPA sample under-represented working-class men more critically than it did men of non-Anglo-Australian background. In both cases there was an implicit assumption by those of us involved that we knew more homosexual behaviour existed among groups, whether defined by class or ethnicity, than was reflected in the survey sample.

Despite the problems of sampling, we are learning that effective HIV/AIDS education affects the ways in which men who have homosexual sex think about themselves. As one New Zealand study concluded:

In order to change their sexual practice, the men first had to acknowledge that they were indeed having sex with other men. The openness required in their relationships with their partners also contributed to making it less possible for them to deny their sexual identity. They could no longer continue to dismiss sex as an 'outlet, bodily function, tension remover' with no bearing on the rest of their lives. (Horn and Chetwynd 1989: 27)

I am not aware of research into either women or men who engage in heterosex which raises the full range of questions in the SAPA study. Indeed, given the absence of a 'heterosexual community' equivalent to the gay, some of the variables revealed by the SAPA studies on community attachment etc., would not be applicable. There are, however, some interesting research projects in Britain, particularly among adolescents (see Aggleton et al. 1990). There is a growing acknowledgment of HIV/AIDS in feminist writing about sexuality, but this has yet to produce much direct impact on research into heterosexual behaviour, with the exception of the work now being undertaken in Australia by Kippax, Crawford, Waldby et al. (1990). Some research on condom usage has been undertaken (Chapman and Hodgson 1988), but there is clearly a need for us to know a lot more about the meanings and conditions connected with the construction of heterosexual relations. As Gagnon has warned:

A narrow view of sexual behaviour may be effective if all we are concerned with is social book keeping and epidemiological modelling, but it will be inadequate to the task of understanding behaviour in a way that results in behaviour change. (Gagnon 1988: 600)

One example: it is my belief that there is far higher acceptance of multiple partners among gay men than most other groups. 'Fidelity' to a relationship does not, for most gay men, require monogamy (Vadasz and Lipp 1990). Ironically, this makes it easier to develop safe sex practices, for couples can admit to themselves that there may be risk of infection from outside liaisons without imperilling the

2 AIDS and the Discourses of Sexuality

entire relationship. Yet we know very little about the ways in which non-monogamous heterosexual relations are negotiated and maintained. Equally we know very little about the impact of pornography, both gay and straight, on the sexual behaviour of those who watch: much gay (but not as much heterosexual) pornography now depicts the use of condoms. Is this in fact eroticising the practice of safe sex? Or should we accept that the depiction of unsafe sex, as is sometimes argued, will be recognized by viewers as fantasy rather than as a guide to conduct in their own lives?

For the most part public policy continues to reflect crude assumptions about 'risk groups' rather than 'risk behaviours'. The best example is that it is still assumed that *all* gay men should observe safe sex guidelines all of the time, even though with growing awareness of HIV-antibody status this is not necessarily the logical conclusion to adopt. This point is often missed in the current discourse about 'relapse' to 'unsafe sex' among gay men (Davies and Project SIGMA 1992). The real need is to persuade those who do not believe they are at risk—and who may not belong, or believe they belong, to 'high risk' groups—to adopt these practices. The more difficult challenge may be to redefine sexuality so that people are willing to see as sexually fulfilling practices which do not necessarily require penetration. The eroticization of massage, masturbation, fantasy, and even sado-masochistic scripts can all be consistent with the promotion of 'safe sex'.

It is not particular sexual practices nor even numbers of sexual partners which are the risk factors for HIV. Rather, there are specific sexual behaviours, which need to be defined in explicit and accurate language. Official 'safe sex' campaigns have sometimes tended to a sort of slippage, whereby they promote monogamy more enthusiastically than safe practices. It might of course be argued that use of condoms can never guarantee 100 per cent safety from HIV transmission: condoms can break, slip off, or be used improperly. (This is the argument for speaking of 'safer' rather than 'safe' sex.) But promoting monogamy, too, as I have already argued, can be misleading. In some ways the most radical approach to 'safe sex' came from sections of the gay community in the promotion of 'Jack-Off' parties—mass sexual encounters where only kissing, fondling and mutual masturbation is allowed (Altman 1985). Such parties arose in San Francisco and New York in the mid-1980s and have now spread widely: Jack-Off (or J/O) parties are a central part of the (limited) preventive education programs for gay men in Paris.

While moralists will be affronted by the glorification of sexual adventure and multiple partners, the idea of the J/O party should reassure those who are concerned that condoms are not always safe and argue that too many of the messages around HIV transmission suggest that the alternative is celibacy or condoms.[3]

J/O parties have been held successfully in Melbourne for several years, but have been far less important in Australia than the United States, partly because gay saunas were never closed in Australia in response to the epidemic, partly because, perhaps, there has been greater belief in the efficacy of condoms here. As the SAPA study reported: 'The main effect of the epidemic on sexuality has been a contraction of the repertoire and a more limited choice of partners, rather than a flowering of sexuality in new (safe) directions ...' (Connell and Kippax 1990: 194).

There is a need to go beyond the J/O concept to explore new possibilities for sexual expression which allow for human contact and experimentation without increasing the risk of HIV transmission. Some writers have suggested that this may lead to a more feminist approach to sex, a downgrading of the emphasis on penetration and orgasm (Albury 1987; Ryan 1987). As Willis wrote:

> If the debate about the appropriate place of condoms in the affairs of society has a positive benefit besides containing the spread of infection, it is likely to be the possibilities for the decline in the male-centred discourse on sexuality, and the emergence and acceptance of female-centred discourse (Willis 1989).

2 AIDS and the Discourses of Sexuality

HOMOPHOBIA AND HETEROSEXISM

As homosexuality has become more and more visible in Western societies it has tended to polarize reactions to it, so that what was once universally condemned becomes a matter for considerable debate within the political arena. Even before the onset of HIV/AIDS those countries which retained legal prohibitions on homosexual behaviour came to debate not only the lifting of these sanctions—a matter of individual and private behaviour—but also prohibition of discrimination based on 'sexual orientation', which implies a social and public definition of homosexuality. In several jurisdictions—New South Wales and Wisconsin at least—this resulted in the anomaly of state protection against discrimination preceding decriminalization of homosexual behaviour (Altman 1982: ch. 4).

Thus the HIV/AIDS debate came on top of a decade at least in which homosexuality had become a politically salient issue in most Western countries. In Australia this probably began with the drowning in Adelaide, South Australia, of a university academic, Dr George Duncan, in 1972 and was carried through in major debates about decriminalization, above all in New South Wales. In the United States it was battles over anti-discrimination ordinances, such as that led by Anita Bryant in Miami in 1977 and State Senator Briggs in California in 1978 which were most significant. HIV/AIDS has had the paradoxical effect of both increasing the legitimacy and the fear of homosexuality: while governments in Australia have funded the largely gay-based AIDS Councils, and included openly gay men on many of their advisory committees, the public perception of HIV infection and AIDS as a 'gay' disease has increased hostility from at least some quarters. This is most dramatically—and tragically—shown in the marked increase in anti-homosexual violence. In recent years 'poofter-bashing' seems to have escalated in our cities, as homosexuals have become both more visible and in some ways, because of HIV/AIDS, a more legitimate target for vigilante violence (Goddard 1991).

To understand the pattern of repressed hatreds and desires which lead young men to beat to death other young men whom they do not know is a major challenge for social research, which requires imaginative researchers able to understand the larger social and cultural contexts within which to evaluate individual behaviour and attitudes. (It may also be one way of thinking about the construction of male heterosexuality, which one researcher at the conference which produced this book termed the 'dark continent'.) Given the extent to which, epidemiologically, AIDS in this country *has* been a 'gay' disease to date, it is remarkable how little research has been concerned with the larger issues of the social context within which homosexuality exists, including that of constant and sometimes violent homophobia. A note on terminology: 'homophobia', a term coined by Weinberg (1972), refers to individual fear of and defence against homosexual desire. I prefer the term 'heterosexism' when one speaks of the whole tissue of social structures, attitudes and organizations which maintain the status of homosexuality as deviant and unacceptable. Both terms apply equally to attitudes towards female as much as male homosexuality.

'Poofter-bashing' (often experienced as viciously by lesbians—or women assumed to be lesbian—as by men assumed to be gay) is a striking example of the sort of problem related to HIV/AIDS which has received virtually no attention from the social research made possible by the epidemic. One of the few studies to examine gay-bashing in the context of the epidemic concluded that:

> Much of the variance in AIDS-related bigotry is explained by anti-gay attitudes which presumably predate the epidemic. Thus AIDS may be less a cause of anti-gay sentiment than a focal event that crystallizes heterosexuals' pre-existing hostility toward gay people. (Herek 1989: 951)

SEXUALITY RESEARCH

In general HIV/AIDS-linked research in Australia has been heavily behavioural, with an almost exclusive emphasis on factors related narrowly to prevention and education. To

2 AIDS and the Discourses of Sexuality

date there has been very little support for the evaluation of cultural meanings and social representations of the sort found in the work of, say, Crimp, Padgug, Singer, Watney, and others (Carter and Watney 1989; Crimp 1988; Padgug 1989; Singer 1989; Treichler 1988b). Missing from our research effort has been the viewpoint of psychoanalysis, of social criticism, of semiotics, above all of cultural anthropology and history. I suspect this is in part a reflection of the traditional scientific paradigms within which HIV/AIDS research has been constructed, above all by the insistence of the Commonwealth AIDS Research Grants Committee upon using the processes and criteria of the National Health and Medical Research Council, and by the lack of real encouragement for research which uses non-positivist paradigms.

While considerable work has now been undertaken on sexual behaviours, and some on the meanings attributed to those practices by individuals, we have very little real understanding of the intersection of public discourse and representation on the one hand, and sexual behaviour and fantasies on the other. In terms of the requirements for HIV/AIDS prevention it is at least possible that the messages about sexual behaviour contained in mass market television and movies far outweigh those of specific media campaigns, which suggest quite different strategies to those which have been adopted. These need not, it is important to note, mean a restrictive sexual morality of the sort now being pushed in the 'new monogamy' of some Hollywood films. Rather we need find ways of incorporating 'safe sex' messages into television series, such as 'Neighbours', 'E Street' and 'Home and Away', just as they are in those few movies ('Big Business' and 'Pretty Woman') where characters are depicted buying condoms before going out on dates. (Some television series *have* depicted AIDS, but I am not aware of any in Australia which regularly promote the message that sex with a number of partners is acceptable, but is a choice that carries certain risks and certain obligations.)

The very ways in which HIV/AIDS is changing popular discourses as well as practices is surely worthy of intellectual study, which would recognize, as Robert Padgug argued, that: '[AIDS] is the product of multiple historical determinations involving the complex social interaction of human beings over time. It is not, as the National Academy of Sciences would have it, "the story of a virus" ' (Padgug 1989: 293). In particular, there is a need for studies that involve a complex engagement with theoretical issues, rather than, as seems to be true of most current research projects, an almost total concentration on immediate applied issues. The SAPA studies suggest that the best practical research can grow out of a recognition of theoretical complexity, in particular out of an attempt to grapple with the problematic, diverse and tentative ways in which humans construct their sexuality.

Moreover, HIV/AIDS has enabled the funding of some community-based projects around sexuality which have in turn produced considerable additions to our knowledge of sexuality: for example, some of the work being done by sex-worker groups, and the varied peer-education projects which exist among gay men (Parnell 1989). There are now some exciting possibilities in Australia for 'action–research', which would acknowledge the role of social movements in creating new discourses and communities around sexuality. In particular, there is a great need to enable interaction between researchers and practitioners to develop ways of reflecting upon and writing up the considerable insights and information about human sexuality which have arisen out of prevention education programs generated by attempts to prevent the spread of HIV.

A NEW SEXUALITY MORALITY?

In the first few years of the HIV epidemic it seemed as if the most likely impact of the new disease would be to promote a fundamentalist return to 'traditional' sexual morality, in which promiscuity, homosexuality and prostitution could all be proscribed in the name of public health. Certainly there are many examples of attempts to use HIV/AIDS to promote this agenda: New South Wales Legislative Councillor (and morals campaigner) Fred Nile's

2 AIDS and the Discourses of Sexuality

attacks on the Gay and Lesbian Mardi Gras, the frequent pronouncements of Catholic Church leaders about the sinfulness of condom use, the strange images of the newly chaste James Bond. Some of this new sexual conservatism pre-dated the HIV epidemic (Altman 1986: 171–3), but it was undoubtedly given a new boost by the threat of a sexually transmissible fatal disease. But prophecies that 'AIDS could herald an almost universal return to monogamy [and] even celibacy' (Mooney 1984), now seem remarkably naive. As we enter the end of the first decade of living with HIV/AIDS it seems that in this country at least HIV/AIDS has expanded rather than contracted sexual expression, although in a far more complex way than might have been imagined in the liberationist rhetoric of the early 1970s.

I would end where I began: one of the crucial impacts of HIV/AIDS has been on the ways in which we think about, talk about and, increasingly, act out sexuality. The impact is most dramatic in the area of male homosexuality, but it extends far beyond that. When ACT UP, an HIV/AIDS radical activist organization, staged a 'kiss-in' in Melbourne's Bourke Street Mall in December 1990 to oppose the 'degaying' of World AIDS Day, the participants included many lesbians. Talk of 'safe sex' that embraces sexual negotiation and sexual adventure is increasingly heard in heterosexual circles. Indeed, the very stress on 'risk behaviours' as a more accurate term than 'risk groups' serves to remind us of the fluidity and artifice of the ways in which we construct sexual identities: it is arguable that HIV/AIDS has simultaneously strengthened a commitment to 'gay community' among very many people, while also reminding us that identities and communal allegiances are ultimately human constructions and, therefore, never immutable.

I have suggested elsewhere that the gay/lesbian movement has been successful in Australia to the extent that it has been able to portray homosexuals as akin to an ethnic group and hence deserving of minimum legitimacy and resourcing as part of the official commitment to multiculturalism (Altman 1989). This development seems to have been hastened by HIV/AIDS rather than retarded, in spite of some of the attempts of the fundamentalist right. Certainly the Australian response to HIV/AIDS has been remarkable in the extent to which it has involved government recognition of and support for gay organizations and gay participation in prevention, support and policy work (Altman 1991). As this occurs it becomes easier for people to conceive that sexuality allows for a variety of expressions and institutions; it may be a long jump from state government funding for a Gay Men's Community Health Centre (a program of the Victorian AIDS Council) to the realization of gay liberation ideals, but there is a connection. Equally, the frankness about heterosex contained in at least some of the official messages about HIV/AIDS prevention suggests a break with part of the wowser tradition of Australian society. After the HIV epidemic sexuality in general, but homosexuality in particular, is very unlikely to be forced back into the closet of respectable prudery and hypocrisy.

NOTES

[1] The relevant literature would require a major bibliographic essay. Good starting points in Australia are the columns of Adam Carr in *Outrage* (Melbourne) and, in Britain, the work of Simon Watney in a range of gay publications.

[2] There is a growing body of relevant literature on the varied social shapes of homosexuality: in Brazil, see Parker (1990); in Thailand, see Jackson (1989).

[3] I am very doubtful whether J/O parties, with their strong emphasis on both exhibitionism and voyeurism, would work in a heterosexual setting. As Pronger observes:

> The difference between homosexual and heterosexual voyeurism is substantial. The power difference of the gender myth always puts women at risk in their relations with men; rape is an ever-present fear for women. Men, on the other hand, are virtually never raped by women, and very seldom by gay men (they are, however, often raped by straight men in prisons and other all-male environments). (Pronger 1990: 205)

3

'THE UNCLEAN MOTION OF THE GENERATIVE PARTS': FRAMEWORKS IN WESTERN THOUGHT ON SEXUALITY

R. W. Connell and G. W. Dowsett

INTRODUCTION

Sexuality is a major theme in our culture, from the surf video to the opera stage to the papal encyclical. It is, accordingly, one of the major themes of the human sciences, and figures as weighty as Darwin and Freud have made major contributions to it. Social research has, over the last hundred years, produced crucially important evidence for the understanding of sexuality. But social *theory* has been slow to grapple with the issue, to give it the sophisticated attention that has been devoted to questions of production or of communication.

We are convinced that an adequate social theory of sexuality is essential for progress on 'applied' issues, such as the design of research on the social transmission of human immunodeficiency virus (HIV). This chapter attempts a mapping exercise, sorting out the major intellectual frameworks that have governed Western thinking about sexuality. We discuss first the religious and scientific nativism that dominated the field into the twentieth century, the problems this approach ran into, and the rise of social construction approaches to sexuality. We discuss the impasse that social constructionism has reached. In the final part of the chapter we sketch the outline of an approach which can move past these difficulties.

Covering such a large issue in a short time necessitates taking a fairly broad approach. But we hope to give enough of the key details to show the practical significance of theoretical frameworks.

NATIVISM

At the bedrock of our culture's thinking about sexuality is the assumption that a given pattern of sexuality is native to the human constitution. We will call this position 'nativism'. It has much in common with what others call 'essentialism', but we want to stress the assumption about origin. Whether laid down by God, achieved by evolution, or settled by the hormones, the nativist assumption is that sexuality is fundamentally *pre-social*. Whatever society does, in attempts to control, channel or restrict, cannot alter the fundamentals of sexuality.

Until quite recently in Western culture nativism was mainly expressed in religious terms. In the ascetic Christian tradition sexuality was read as 'lust'. It was part of the old Adam, an aspect of fallen humanity to be wrestled with and defeated. As Saint Augustine, no stranger to the pleasures of the flesh, put it:

> Although therefore there may be many lusts, yet when we read the word 'lust' alone without mention of the object, we commonly take it for the unclean motion of the generative parts. For this holds sway in the whole body, moving the whole man, without and within, with such a mixture of mental emotion and carnal appetite that hence is the highest bodily pleasure of all produced: so that in the very moment of consummation, it overwhelms almost all of the light and power of cogitation ... Justly is man ashamed of this lust, and justly are those members (which lust moves or suppresses against our wills, as it lusts) called shameful. (*City of God* XIV, xvi–xvii)

This outlook was institutionalized in monasticism. (Augustine himself was involved in the very early days of the monastic movement.) Chastity as an ideal spread beyond the monasteries. Thus an attack on married priests was a major feature of Pope Gregory VII's church reforms in the eleventh century. In a process that prefigures a more recent

3 'The Unclean Motion of the Generative Parts'

sexual politics, sexuality became an arena for the assertion of other agendas. The attack on priestly marriage occurred in the context of an assertion of the centralized power of the papacy and its attempts to control the priesthood more generally (Greenberg 1988: 290–2).

Resistance to asceticism, a reassertion of the flesh, correspondingly arose in the form of anticlericalism and irreligious humour. The classic expressions were the songs of the wandering scholars and the bawdy tales of the *Decameron*. As the medieval Archpoet put it in his *Confession* (1952):

> Wounded to the quick am I
> By a young girl's beauty:
> She's beyond my touching? Well,
> Can't the mind do duty?
>
> Hard beyond all hardness, this
> Mastering of Nature:
> Who shall say his heart is clean,
> Near so fair a creature?
>
> Young are we, so hard a law,
> How should we obey it?
> And our bodies, they are young,
> Shall they have no say in't?
>
> Sit you down amid the fire,
> Will the fire not burn you?
> To Pavia come, will you
> Just as chaste return you?

Yet another strand in Christian thought affirmed the flesh in the service of God. No less a figure than Martin Luther, the married monk, stands for this view. The mainstream Protestant concept of Christian marriage has offered a picture of legitimate lust, flowing in channels divinely ordained. Here, sexuality was not condemned as such but divided between the territory of God and the terrain of the Devil. In this splitting we can see the remote roots of the image of the sexual 'other' which has haunted the modern Western imagination from Don Juan, the villain of Mozart's operatic stage, to 'Patient Zero', the media villain of the HIV epidemic in the United States (Shilts 1987).

In the later nineteenth century religious nativism began to be displaced as our culture's main account of sexuality. What replaced it was scientific nativism. Darwin's *Descent of Man*, published in 1874, marks the shift. This offered a detailed account of 'sexual selection' which Darwin now emphasized alongside 'natural selection' as a mechanism of evolution. Sexual attraction was firmly located in the order of nature and indeed given a steering role in organic evolution.

Only twelve years later Krafft-Ebing in Austria published *Psychopathia Sexualis*, the marker of scientific nativism applied to humans. This was essentially a scientization of the image of the 'sexual other'. Using medical and legal records Krafft-Ebing catalogued and classified, like a horrified butterfly collector, the many types of sexual degeneracy. His catch-all explanation of sexual otherness was 'hereditary taint'. As well as deploying a natural science rhetoric he attempted to deploy natural science methods. For instance in his case study of the 'Countess in male attire' he attempted anthropometrics. After measuring everything from her ear/chin line (26.5 cm) to her vagina, which was too narrow for the 'insertion of a membrum virile', he concluded her congenital sexual inversion 'expressed itself, anthropologically, in anomalies of the development of the body, depending on great hereditary taint' (1965: 437–8).

The type of scientificity was redefined, but the basic claim could only be reinforced, when sexology moved out of a forensic into a clinical context. The Western *scientia sexualis*, which Foucault (1978: 57) has tellingly contrasted with the erotic lore of other cultures, reached its first climax when Freud's key volumes appeared in 1900 and 1905, and Ellis's in 1897. Freud developed a flexible but profound therapeutic and research technique; he produced also a detailed developmental model of human sexuality, bringing childhood sexuality into focus. His most influential arguments demonstrated the protean character of sexual motivation and the significance of sexuality for human

3 'The Unclean Motion of the Generative Parts'

psychology generally. Ellis added a more sympathetic documentation of the range of sexual practices and the forms of life that might be built around them.

Across the Atlantic, the monuments of American sexology in the twentieth century sustained the claim to scientificity. Kinsey was a zoologist by training (a specialist in gall wasps), and regarded his massive interview studies of human sexuality as an extension of biology. When the twin storms of fundamentalist religious denunciation and media salacity broke over his head, it was to his identity as a scientist that Kinsey clung for salvation (Pomeroy 1972). (It is worth remembering, in the light of current debates about research funding in Australia, that Kinsey *did* have his research grants cut off after his work had become politically embarrassing.)

Masters and Johnson, working in a school of medicine, had a more clinical style and claimed to be even more nativist than Kinsey:

> Although the Kinsey work has become a landmark of sociologic investigation [certainly not how Kinsey saw it], it was not designed to interpret physiologic or psychologic response to sexual stimulation. [In fact Kinsey's group did such research but kept it secret.] Those *fundamentals of human sexual behaviour* [our emphasis] cannot be established until two questions are answered: What physical reactions develop as the human male and female respond to effective sexual stimulation? Why do men and women behave as they do when responding to effective sexual stimulation? (1966: 3–4)

The irony of attempting to answer these universally stated questions by a study of 382 female and 312 male white heterosexual upper-status midwestern urban Americans in their twenties and thirties has not been lost on critics. Nevertheless Masters and Johnson produced a result which has a claim to be the only research finding in all sexology which has no social significance at all. During sexual excitement the vaginal walls of their female subjects changed colour, and changed back again ten or fifteen minutes later (1966: 75, 79). The only social question of interest here is why someone would be watching.

The work on homosexuality by the same research group highlights the extent to which social relationships and social meanings are excised in the pursuit of scientificity. For instance, the foreplay of heterosexual and homosexual couples, fellatio/cunnilingus, masturbation, anal intercourse and other activities are compared as if these were purely technical performances (Masters and Johnson 1970). That anal intercourse, for one, is relationally quite a different matter for heterosexual and homosexual couples in American culture is an issue that does not arise.

With Masters and Johnson scientific nativism, considered as a paradigm or research program in the sense of Kuhn (1962) and Lakatos (1970), is in full collapse. Far from offering an expanding program of investigation, a way of talking about sexuality in its fullness, such research is only able to operate by fencing off a small corner of the field. It may call this corner the 'fundamentals', but this is rhetoric. The research itself does not provide a path by which we may account for 'the rest' in terms of these fundamentals. Within a few years two veterans of Kinsey's institute, Gagnon and Simon, would point to the 'non-cumulative' character of research in naturalistic sexology (1974: 7) and commit themselves to a decisively different framework based on a kind of sociology.

The flaws in scientific nativism are clear enough in retrospect. It has never come to terms with one of the key bodies of evidence on human sexuality built up in the last hundred years, the anthropologists' documentation of massive cross-cultural variation in sexual practice (Marshall and Suggs 1971). It has not even been able to account for sexual variation within its own culture—despite many futile studies attempting to find a physiological basis for male or female homosexuality (Wakeling 1979). What Freud called 'object choice' remains a mystery to sexology. The guiding metaphor of scientific nativism, that the body and its natural processes provide a 'base' or 'foundation' which determines the superstructure of social relations, in fundamental ways misrepresents the relationships between bodies and social processes. This issue is taken up again in the final section.

The nativist discourse is curiously silent on two issues which pervade representations of sexuality in literature, art

3 'The Unclean Motion of the Generative Parts'

and music: desire and pleasure. The closest that nativism comes to the concept of desire is the idea of a sex 'drive' or, in Freud's term, 'libido'. This is a force compelling effects, an urge or impulse to behaviour—a more or less uncontrollable one in some accounts going back to Augustine's. It is difficult to connect this to the kind of experience recalled by our poets and writers, that sharp intake of breath as light falls unexpectedly on a breast or buttock, or the memory of a first kiss:

> at first
> a feeling like
> silk, then
> a slight motion
> of lip on lip
> and breathing
> I take your
> lower lip
> into my mouth,
> delight
> in its blood-round
> softness, re-
> lease it, we kiss,
> your tongue
> explores; for
> the first time
> it touches mine:
> tip and surface,
> root and vein,
> our eyes open. (Peters 1973)

Pleasure is equally remote in a discourse of nerve endings, engorged vesicles, muscular spasm. The imaginative dimension in enjoyment, the creative search for erotic pleasures, is put firmly in its place:

> Epstein (1960) argued that some of the behaviors of fetishists resemble the symptoms of temporal lobe dysfunction . . . [However] He has advanced no physiological evidence to directly point to temporal lobe dysfunction in fetishists. (Lester 1975: 162–3)

Again the approach is curiously lacking in a grasp of, or even reference to, human experience. Scientific nativism has lost its grasp of the most important subject-matter. Even de Sade, in his extraordinary catalogues of libertinage and violence, managed to survey sexual capacity, diversity and perversity with considerable attention to pleasure (de Sade 1785/1966).

Though nativism is dead as a scientific program, it remains powerful as social ideology. Here religion and natural science are in unexpected alliance to support social 'common sense': boys need to sow their wild oats, rapists may be caught but rape can not be stopped, girls naturally want to look beautiful and to have babies, lesbianism is unnatural . . . The half-scientific, half-demonological concept of 'the pervert' is an active one, as current politics shows. Consider the persistent attempts of New South Wales politicians in 1989–90 (continuing at the time of writing) to mobilize hatred of 'child molesters' in the aftermath of the legal vindication of the accused in the so-called 'Mr Bubbles' case.

A less dramatic but telling example of nativist ideology is the treatment of transsexuals in the prison system. Though placing male-to-female transsexuals in a men's prison places them at acute risk of rape and bashing, it has proved difficult to get official agreement to place them in women's prisons. The chromosomes rule; more exactly, a biological warrant is found for pre-existing social ideology.

'FRAME' THEORIES: THE SOCIAL CONSTRUCTION OF SEXUALITY

The view that sexuality is shaped by society was stated with particular clarity by Gagnon and Simon (1974), who developed the image of sexual conduct as the enactment of social 'scripts':

> It is the authors' contention . . . that all human sexual behavior is socially scripted behavior. The sources of sexual arousal are to be found in socio-cultural definitions, and it is extremely difficult to conceive of any type of human sexual activity without this definitional aspect . . . It is not the physical aspects

3 'The Unclean Motion of the Generative Parts'

of sexuality but the social aspects that generate the arousal and organize the action. (1974: 262)

Such a viewpoint had been developing for a good while before it was so clearly stated. Indeed its origins go back at least to Freud. Freud's general framework was solidly nativist. He saw himself as a natural scientist and physician, he took a reductionist view of psychology, and his conception of the sexual drive or instinct was developed on the analogy of physiological needs. Yet Freud's psychiatric practice, his case studies, and his specific theorization of psychosexual development (particularly in the *Three Essays* of 1905), all undermined the reductionist framework.

Though most discussions of Freud's sexual science emphasize the abstract theory, we would emphasize the case studies, the core of psychoanalysis as he saw it. With astonishing delicacy—given his cultural context—Freud documented the role played by social relationships, especially those within the family, in the shaping of the sexual–emotional life of his patients. Here was the first, and in some ways still the most powerful, evidence for some crucially important conclusions. Freud demonstrated that actual sexualities are not received as a package from biology; that adult sexuality is arrived at by a highly variable and observable process of construction, not by an 'unfolding' of the natural; and that social process is deeply implicated in this construction.

Freud's oscillation between nativist presumptions and constructionist insights has remained characteristic of psychoanalysis, and psychoanalytic sociology, ever since. Conservative medical psychoanalysis has leaned more to the nativist side, and psychoanalytic radicals have leaned more to the constructionist, but the tension has remained. Thus Reich (1972), who had a more vivid understanding than any other psychoanalytic theorist of the pressures placed by class oppression on working-class sexuality, never abandoned his belief in the naturalness of heterosexuality. Dinnerstein (1976), by contrast, sees heterosexuality as necessarily abrasive and discordant, as a result of its construction through the gendered parenting practices which pervade Western societies. Marcuse (1955) developed a classic analysis of the social bases of the bodily organization of sexual pleasure, the pressures leading towards genital primacy and the focusing of sexuality on procreation. Yet he was so convinced of the importance of the organic basis of sexual desire that he found in it the fulcrum for resistance to the repressive social dynamic of advanced capitalism.

A similar ambivalence can be found in classic anthropological works on sexuality. After psychoanalysis, ethnography became during the twentieth century the most important body of evidence requiring a social theory of sexuality. Ethnographers brought back to the European and American intelligentsia accounts of sexual customs so varied but so comprehensible that it was impossible to regard them simply as exotica, as primitivism, or as simple variants on the European pattern. As the Newtonian universe shrank the Earth from being the focus of creation to being merely one of a number of bodies following gravitational laws, so ethnography shrank Western culture from the status of norm, or historic pinnacle, to being one among a large number of comparable cultures which simply had different ways of handling questions of sex.

Yet the ethnographers, confronted with the spectacular variety of sexual custom, persisted in a search for a natural order beneath it. Malinowski, both a pioneer ethnographer of sexuality and a major anthropological theorist, clearly illustrates this. His famous study of the Trobriand Islanders, *The Sexual Life of Savages* (1929), was praised by Ellis as the first serious ethnography of sexuality, placing sexual practices in their full cultural context. It is indeed a richer cultural analysis than anything about *European* sexuality written at the time. But at a theoretical level, in *Sex and Repression in Savage Society* (1927), Malinowski was already hovering between a nativist conception of instinct and a theory of the shaping of emotion by a 'sociological mechanism'. Sexuality appears in this text on the border between nature and culture. As Malinowski's functionalist theory of culture matured, the nativist underpinnings became more explicit. The account of institutions was now

3 'The Unclean Motion of the Generative Parts'

based on a statement of 'the biological foundations of culture'. The sequence 'sex appetite → conjugation → detumescence' was one of eleven 'permanent vital sequences incorporated in all cultures'. Kinship institutions were the cultural response to a social need for reproduction (1960 [1944]: 75–103). The various sexual customs were thus particular ways in which cultures solved common problems of naturally-given human need, each making sense within the *Gestalt* of its own culture. The culture provided context for the resolution of natural need.

Gagnon and Simon's sociology of sex pushed further the tradition which we will call 'frame' theories of sexuality. Gagnon and Simon's version is an adaptation of role theory, the approach in sociology that locates the constraints on behaviour in the stereotyped expectations held by other social actors (Connell 1979). Individuals internalize these normative expectations or enact them under the threat of social sanctions; in Gagnon and Simon's metaphor, they follow social scripts. Much of *Sexual Conduct* is a heroic attempt to spell out the scripts. Most notable is the grand script of a lifelong sexual career in contemporary Western culture (1974: 99–103). Gagnon and Simon also attempt to decipher the scripts for homosexual women and men, for youth, for prostitutes and for prisoners.

Read as radical in its day, this now appears a curiously unfocused exercise. The reason is that Gagnon and Simon's framework provides no *social* account of what links the diverse scripts together, what makes them all 'sexuality'. Nor is the unity within a script very clear. The framework does not account for progress along the career path, how we are moved from stage to stage. One eventually realizes that this self-consciously social account has a non-social centre. What defines a matter as 'sexual' is in fact the biology of arousal and reproduction. Gagnon and Simon's sociology does not displace Masters and Johnson's natural history. It provides a social frame for their subject matter. The corner has become a centre; and the scope of the frame is defined by a backward movement from that centre.

Foucault's theorizing provides a social account of the unity of 'sexuality', and in that regard is the pinnacle of the social framing account. As a cultural historian and post-structuralist philosopher, Foucault came from a very different intellectual background from Gagnon and Simon. But he insists as strongly on rejecting nativism and asserting the social. 'The social' here is more concrete than a set of social expectations or scripts. It is a set of historically describable discourses which, operating in professions and state apparatuses, *constitute* 'sexuality' as an object of knowledge and social concern:

> Sexuality must not be thought of as a kind of natural given which power tries to hold in check, or as an obscure domain which knowledge tries gradually to uncover. It is the name that can be given to a historical construct: not a furtive reality that is difficult to grasp, but a great surface network in which the stimulation of bodies, the intensification of pleasures, the incitement to discourse, the formation of special knowledges, the strengthening of controls and resistances, are linked to one another, in accordance with a few major strategies of knowledge and power. (1978: 105–6)

Foucault is particularly scathing about the 'repressive hypothesis' as a guide to the history of sexuality. Against the view of deepening repression and silence about sexuality as modern capitalism developed, he argues that this was precisely the era when discourses of sexuality multiplied, the social incitement to talk about the secrets of sex grew. 'Sexuality' was created as a social fact, a realm for the operation of power (in the sense of social control).

Establishing that control involved an effort to classify and define. The very science of sexuality which its pioneers—most eloquently Ellis—saw as a means of human progress and emancipation, was to Foucault a means of control. The sexual types of which it spoke were constituted as the objects of new strategies of knowledge and control. Foucault's now celebrated list includes the masturbating child, the perverse (principally homosexual) man, the hysterical woman, and the 'Malthusian' couple (1978: 103–5). Here Foucault's argument connects with the important body of historical research which has traced the emergence of 'the homosexual' as a category in Western culture in historically recent times (e.g. Weeks 1977, Bray

3 'The Unclean Motion of the Generative Parts'

1982). The term 'homosexual' itself was coined in the 1860s.

It is significant that this picture of sexuality did not come out of sexology. Rather it came out of a long research program in cultural history in which Foucault had traced the growth of other systems of knowledge, surveillance and control, notably criminology and the prison, medicine and the clinic, psychiatry and the asylum (Foucault 1977, 1973a, 1973b). Focusing closely on systems of control, Foucault left little space for what it is that is being controlled.

'Bodies', certainly; but bodies that seem marked by an unusual passivity in the face of these technologies of power and knowledge. Critics of Foucault have asked where the resistance comes from, if his picture of history is not to be a black night of domination more total than even Marcuse (1968) imagined. Foucault replied that resistance arises at every point in a network of power (1978: 95). But this remains a metaphysical claim in the absence of a substantive account of the generation, articulation and historical organization of resistance. And that Foucault does not supply. Indeed he dismissed the issue with a gibe at the Marcusian idea of a 'great refusal' (1978: 96).

Though Foucault's account of the social frame is markedly more realistic and historically sophisticated than Gagnon and Simon's, there is as great a problem about what holds it together. Foucault's concept of the 'deployment of sexuality' as a strategy of power (1978: 106ff) avoids making the definition of the social process of sexuality dependent on a malleable native 'human sexual response', but it does make the definition dependent on a 'will to knowledge' and a will to power whose social base, location and dynamics remain vague. Where Foucault begins to specify this (1978: 122–7) he does so in surprisingly conventional class terms, as a strategy of bourgeois class formation as well as hegemony. He acknowledged that the (French) working class long escaped the effects of the deployment of sexuality.

Foucault's sudden shift to the language of class is symptomatic of a crisis in social framing theories. Moving away from the physiological concept of sexuality to a focus on the discourses that socially define it leaves an increasingly empty 'frame'. Yet this movement has found no way of conceptualizing the social in terms of sexuality itself. Instead it is obliged to introduce structural and dynamic concepts (class, hegemony, discourse, state) already defined in reference to other historical processes. Sexuality as an object of knowledge and as an object of politics seems to crumble as we look.

The problems this creates are well illustrated by the theoretical difficulties of gay liberation. Deconstructionist ideas, including those of Foucault, had a considerable impact on gay theorists, among them the distinguished British historian Weeks (1985, 1986). Deconstructionist framing theory seemed to give powerful support to themes already important in gay analyses of sexuality. It pointed to the social bases of concepts of normality and deviance, to the pervasiveness of social control, and to the role of professions such as medicine in sustaining control over 'deviants'. The category of 'homosexuality' itself could be seen to be socially constructed by penal laws and medical interpretations.

Here the problems begin. For according to this argument, to claim an identity as a homosexual is to claim a place in a system of social regulation. Yet 'homosexual identity' is the logical basis of homosexual solidarity and the gay movement itself. To resist the identity means to dismantle the movement, leaving no place from which to contest the regulatory power.

The political implications of social construction theory and the deconstructionist reaction to issues of identity were vigorously debated from the end of the 1970s (e.g. Johnston 1981, Sargent 1983). The sense that gay theory had somehow become inimical to gay politics was summed up in reactions recorded in Vance's (1989) useful review of social construction theory: 'deconstruct heterosexuality first!' and 'I'll deconstruct when they deconstruct'. This intellectual climate was perhaps among the centrifugal forces and divergent strategies among homosexual men which, as Pollak (1988) has noted in his study of homosexuals and

3 'The Unclean Motion of the Generative Parts'

HIV/AIDS in France, made it more difficult to organize a collective response to the epidemic.

One of the basic problems in social framing theory is the lack of a definition of sexuality outside the act of scripting or controlling. As Vance (1989: 21) puts it:

> ... to the extent that social construction theory grants that sexual acts, identities and even desire are mediated by cultural and historical factors, the object of the study—sexuality—becomes evanescent and threatens to disappear.

It is understandable that an appeal to nativism may result. There has recently been a revival of a more essentialist position in lesbian and gay analyses of homosexuality (e.g. Williams 1986: ch. 12; Wieringa 1989). Basic forms of sexuality are seen as constant, to some degree, across cultures and periods.

Such a response is given urgency by the attacks on homosexual rights and on recent political gains that have followed the HIV epidemic. HIV infection is an intensely personal and organic condition. Cruel notions of 'innocent' victims versus the others who are infected, or ideas for criminal sanctions to control the epidemic, are reminders of medico-legal sanctions on homosexuality defeated only in the recent past. A neo-essentialist position offers a kind of defence against moral blame. It authenticates experience, particularly body sensations and sexual and emotional responses at the individual level. But by retreating to the individual for basic explanations it loses vital purchase on the social.

If it is not to lapse into a kind of nativism, or into a paradoxical liquidation of the object of knowledge and of social practice, the social analysis of sexuality needs a qualitatively different approach from role theory or deconstructionism. We can say, broadly, what kind of theory is required. It is necessary to find ways of understanding the imbrication of bodies and histories, giving full weight to bodily experience without treating the body as the container of an ahistorical essence of sexuality. It is necessary to find ways of understanding social relations as themselves sexual, not merely as framing sexuality from outside. And it is necessary to understand the coherence and constraint within such relationships. Where role theory collapses structure into action, we need a conceptualization of social structure in the domain of sexual practice.

FROM THE SOCIAL CONSTRUCTION OF SEXUALITY TO THE SEXUAL CONSTRUCTION OF SOCIETY

To resolve the political dilemma of deconstruction in the face of the enemy, and the conceptual problem of the absent centre in social constructionism, are two problems that require the same approach. Rather than moving back towards nativism, we need to move further into the social, developing an account of sexuality which is *fully* social and can stand on its own as social analysis.

Not even Freud, for all his emphasis on Eros, developed a concept of sexuality as social structure. When he tried to sociologize psychoanalysis (notably in *Civilization and its Discontents*) the social constraint upon Eros came from vaguely specified imperatives of technological development and social order (1930). The breakthrough came with 'second-wave' feminism and gay liberation—and then it came with a rush. Within ten years a whole battery of linked, though by no means equivalent, concepts had been proposed.

Millett's (1972) concept of 'sexual politics' struck to the heart of the matter, announcing from the start that questions about sexuality were questions about power. Her book explored the way sexual relationships in the work of certain novelists became a form of domination of women by men. We might now take a more complex view of the relation between text and practice. But the insight into power, which Millett shared with others in the first years of the women's liberation movement (Willis 1984), is still basic.

In the first years of the gay liberation movement the point was taken further. Sexuality involves relations of power within genders as well as between them. Though using a similar terminology of oppression (Altman 1972, Johnston 1981), the focus here was on differences of identity as much

3 'The Unclean Motion of the Generative Parts'

as on relations of subordination. The idea of multiple sexualities with a complex of social relationships between them readily follows from this. The 1970s indeed saw a multiplication of sexual personae in gay and lesbian milieux, from androgynes and drag queens to leather dykes and clones. But diversity did not mean disintegration. These presentations of sexuality were also involved in the construction of modern visible gay communities, which appear to people outside as homogeneous.

Since the new feminism took some years to come to terms with lesbianism, these two arguments did not immediately merge. They were eventually brought together in a striking way by Rich (1980), who turned the social construction of deviance argument on its head and argued the social construction of heterosexuality. 'Compulsory heterosexuality', she proposed, was a political institution, requiring women to be sexually available to men and sustaining their dependence on men. Rich contrasted this with a 'lesbian continuum' of relationships among women independent of men, including erotic relationships but also friendship, work, child care and so on. Her handling of the theme is ahistorical, but the idea is useful in dramatizing the scale on which social relationships may be organized through sexuality.

A significantly different approach to sexuality was taken in Mitchell's now somewhat neglected *Woman's Estate* (1971), under the influence of structuralist Marxism. Mitchell was concerned to distinguish the different sites of women's oppression, on the assumption that relationships in different sites might follow different historical trajectories and give rise to differently configured political struggles. 'Sexuality' figured in her theorizing as one of the four 'structures' of women's oppression, alongside production, reproduction and the socialization of children.

It is not difficult to see the logical incoherence of this framework, and Mitchell herself did not persist with it for long. Yet the moment is important. This text is where sexuality is *named* as a domain of social structure in its own right, alongside and interacting with other social structures, and requiring its own mapping as structure.

Curiously, Mitchell's second essay in structural analysis (1974) was a considerable retreat from this prospect of a structural history of sexuality. The model of 'structure' was now drawn from Lévi-Strauss's essentially ahistorical anthropology. Sexuality became the means by which persons are inserted into kinship and gender structures. The analysis of affect was greatly expanded, but separated from the analysis of structure. Mitchell's later work moved back towards orthodox psychoanalysis.

In a key paper by Rubin (1975) the idea of sexuality as social structure received a clear definition:

> ... they [Freud and Lévi-Strauss] provide conceptual tools with which one can build descriptions of the part of social life which is the locus of the oppression of women, of sexual minorities, and of certain aspects of human personality within individuals. I call that part of life the 'sex/gender system', for lack of a more elegant term. As a preliminary definition, a 'sex/gender system' is a set of arrangements by which a society transforms biological sexuality into products of human activity, and in which these transformed sexual needs are satisfied. (159)

Though Rubin maintains a concept of biological capacity and need, she is emphatic that actual sexuality is historically produced:

> Sex as we know it—gender identity, sexual desire and fantasy, concepts of childhood—is itself a social product. We need to understand the relations of its production. (166)

As this phrasing suggests, the content of the 'sex/gender system' is twofold. On the one hand there is the socially-produced *domain* of practice. On the other hand are the *social relations* organizing that domain, which take different structural forms in different societies or periods of history. Rubin draws much from Lévi-Strauss here, but also argues for going beyond kinship to a 'political economy of sexual systems' (177, 204–10) drawing on Marxist concepts about production systems.

The territory opened up by this conceptual work in the 1970s has been developed in three bodies of research, which inflect in slightly different ways the basic idea of social relations constituted in or through sexuality. The first

3 'The Unclean Motion of the Generative Parts'

pursues the political economy of sex through studies of sexuality in workplaces. A notable example is Pringle's (1988) study of secretaries. Pringle demonstrates that sexuality is not an optional extra in office life, nor something that starts and finishes with the Christmas cocktail party. It is intricately interwoven with routine labour processes in a quite inescapable way. Sexuality is part of the way boss/secretary relationships are *constituted*.

One of the most striking things in Pringle's book is the demonstration that this holds whether or not there is the kind of behaviour that Kinsey would count as a sexual act, or a court would count as sexual harassment. And it holds regardless of the gender of the boss (though with a female boss the configuration of sexuality is different). Sexual pleasure and unpleasure is part of the ordinary motivational structure of office life. A similar conclusion pushed Hearn and Parkin (1987), working on what they call 'organization sexuality', to reconsider their initial understanding of the topic:

> We have found it necessary to broaden our definition in at least two ways: firstly, to see sexuality as an ordinary and frequent public process rather than an extraordinary and predominantly private process; and secondly, to see sexuality as an aspect and part of an all-pervasive body politics rather than a separate and discrete set of practices. Thus the term sexuality is used here specifically to refer to the social expression of or social relations to physical, bodily desires, real or imagined, by or for others or for oneself. (1987: 57–8)

The theme of 'imagined' relations is central to the second body of work on the symbolic dimension of sexuality. This takes off from the fertile encounter of semiotics and psychoanalysis in the work of Kristeva and others. Previous work on media and culture had debated the way sexuality is governed by discourse (a familiar example is the debates about the effects of pornography—Lockhart et al. 1970). What was at issue now was the way sexuality is constitutive of symbolism and language.

Kristeva herself (1984) saw the very possibility of language as rooted in psychosexual development. If true this would open the whole domain of human communication to analysis in terms of sexual social relations. By extension, sexual theory would be required to understand all the decentred social forms spoken of by post-modernists to whom 'the social bond is linguistic' (Lyotard 1984).

More specifically there is a semiotics of sexuality, in which relationships of acceptance and expulsion, identity and difference, possession and domination, are established (e.g. Burgin et al. 1986). Much feminist work on sexual 'difference' (Eisenstein and Jardine 1980) operates at the level of symbolism and meanings, where sexual differences are sharp, rather than at the level of personality and interpersonal practice, where differences are much slighter that is usually believed (Epstein 1988).

The process of constructing sexual meanings is particularly clearly shown by recent work on the cultural dimensions of the HIV epidemic—an 'epidemic of signification' as Treichler (1988a) wittily put it. In what Watney (1988) calls 'the spectacle of AIDS' we can see at a particular historical moment how social relations of dominance are asserted through the generation of sexual meanings.

The third body of research reworks the terrain once visited by Malinowski and Mead. Mead (1949) classically formulated the cross-cultural study of sex and gender as a standard human nature finding varied cultural expression. Mead argued that the making of the 'social personalities of the two sexes' was a social process, a matter of a cultural template being placed over the natural variability of temperament (Mead 1935). But her argument became deeply confused about the role of innate differences—which she was convinced existed both within and between the sexes—and their interaction with the *Gestalt* of a culture. Ultimately Mead wished to proclaim the common humanity underlying cultural difference—a radical enough message in the era of Fascism and late colonialism—and this had the effect of domesticating her ethnography and tying her to a philosophical nativism.

By contrast the new anthropology of sexuality has emphasized the genuine alienness of other culture's sexual arrangements. Herdt (1981), in the study which has done more than any other to establish this approach, describes

3 'The Unclean Motion of the Generative Parts'

a Papua-New Guinea culture which violates the cross-cultural assumption of heterosexuality as norm and homosexuality as minority practice. In this culture homosexual practice is virtually universal among men, and is not only tolerated but ritually insisted upon at certain stages of the life cycle. In a range of other Melanesian cultures too, it can be shown that same-sex erotic contact is socially required in certain contexts, is part of the routine ritual work of the society (Herdt 1984).

To use the category of 'the homosexual' to describe the people involved, or 'homosexuality' as a name for their practice, would be to impose an alien frame of reference that would make nonsense of the behaviour as situated, meaningful practice. Similarly Parker et al. (1989) have argued, in the context of the HIV epidemic, that North American notions of 'homosexuality' are inappropriate as a basis for health promotion strategies for Brazilian men who have sex with men. HIV/AIDS prevention models developed in Europe and North America equally misconstrue male-to-male sex in South-east Asia. This point applies to Australia, where assumptions are often made in research and education that all men who have sex with men are 'gay' or 'homosexual' and a standard meaning is read into those terms.

We learn from these anthropological accounts that the structures of sexual relationships, and the social categories constituted through them, are not uniform from one society to another. They are historically produced. In the ethnographer's telescope we can see more dramatically, because of the alienness of the categories and the practices, something that is also true of our own society. Erotic contact is part of a process of relationship-making, of society-making. The Czech philosopher Kosik (1976) nicely described human praxis as 'onto-formative', constitutive of the reality we live in. This is true of sexuality as social practice also.

In this section we have attempted to move beyond the idea of structure as a determining frame which is characteristic of both structuralist and post-structuralist approaches; beyond even the idea of a frame in motion. Sexuality is more that a domain in which history is enacted.

It is constitutive of history itself. Society does not simply construct sexuality, society is constructed sexually. Once this is accepted we cannot be content with images of moulding, regulating, controlling. We must think of sexuality in terms of historically dynamic patternings of practice and relationship, which have considerable scope and power.

GROWTH POINTS FOR THEORY

The previous section attempted to state the logical shape of the next step in theory, and outlined the bodies of research requiring it. We now turn to some of the problems the construction of such an approach faces.

The theoretical work of the last two decades has established the need for, and the possibility of, an analysis of the structure of relationships constituted through sexual practice. But it has certainly not arrived at anything like agreement on what this structure is. Two main possibilities exist.

First, an account of structure in sexuality can be built on the approach in social theory that emphasizes the mutual implication of structure and practice, but does not reject a structuralist account of structure per se (cf. Giddens 1984). Thus Connell (1987: 111–16) offers an account of sexuality centring on the social relation of emotional attachment. This account suggests that in our culture a highly visible structure, characterized by gender oppositions and couple relationships, coexists with a 'shadow' structure detectable in the ambivalence of major relationships. This ambivalence is a theme developed by Dinnerstein (1976) in particular.

An alternative approach moves away from this concept of structure to analyse the social as the intersection and interplay of a multiplicity of discourses, symbolic systems or language games (Weedon 1987). This would lead to a more fragmented and multi-levelled account of sexualities (e.g. Coward 1984). This approach yields some gain in the capacity to theorize tension and transition. But it has less capacity to grasp large-scale issues such as those involved in the impact of Western on non-Western sexual cultures.

3 'The Unclean Motion of the Generative Parts'

One of the main advantages that social construction theories of sexuality had over nativism and individualism is that they offered a way of accounting for the sexual categories present at a particular moment in history (which nativism takes to be pre-ordained) and for the sexual options available in a given setting to the individual (which profoundly shape the choice, however free the act of choosing may be). Fascinating historical work has been done on the making of such categories as the homosexual man (McIntosh 1968, Weeks 1977, Bray 1982), the prostitute (Walkowitz 1980, Allen 1990b), the housewife (Game and Pringle 1979).

The sophistication of this historical work has not, however, been matched by a theoretical capacity to analyse the process by which new sexual categories are generated. This lack is disturbing, since history has not quite come to an end. We can see in the culture around us, beyond the signs of changing styles in sexuality, evidence of the production of whole new categories.

The *transsexual* is clearly being produced as a new social category, despite the fervent wish of most people in it to disappear into the taken-for-granted categories of 'woman' or 'man' (Bolin 1988). A clear indication is the emergence of a market for the services of transsexual prostitutes (Perkins 1983). The *paedophile* is also perhaps on the way from being a category in forensic psychiatry to being a character in popular culture. The word itself is now used in journalism, presupposing a much wider recognition of the sexual 'type' than could have been presumed even ten years ago. Indeed the title is being claimed by paedophiles themselves (O'Carroll 1982); both to separate themselves from homosexuals, and also to claim, in a classic sexual liberation-inspired way, the contested ground from those who would regulate them, namely the state.

In HIV/AIDS policy the production of categories takes the form of a medical discourse of 'risk groups'. The conceptual muddle produced by blurring practices into groups can be seen in the monthly *Australian HIV Surveillance Reports*, where there is an HIV transmission category entitled 'Homosexual/Bisexual'. Logically there is no such thing as bisexual transmission of HIV, unless a man is having simultaneous anal and/or vaginal intercourse with a man and a woman, both of them are already infected, and they infect him at the same moment!

The key to an understanding of the production of categories is a concept of collective agency. 'Agency' is most commonly thought of as a property of the individual person. The couples 'agency/determination', 'practice/structure' are thus assimilated to the opposition 'individual/society'.

Yet agency in sexual matters is often a question of the historical creation and mobilization of collectivities. Witness the mobilization of women's agency in relation to sexuality (marriage and contraception for instance) around the turn of the century traced by Magarey (1985). A more recent example is the mobilization of homosexual men achieved by the gay liberation movement in the 1970s, and the 'safe sex' movement itself in the 1980s.

Collectivities may of course mean institutions, as well as social movements. Thus one may recognize the historical effect of a company, a market, or the state. The case of HIV/AIDS 'risk groups' illustrates the effect of the institutions of medicine and their ways of categorizing the world. The idea of multiple collectivities—as distinct from multiple subjectivities or even intersubjectivity—allows far more room for politics in the operation of structure. Regulation and contestation become more observable and, in one sense, more concrete.

An irony of social framing theory is its tendency to lose the body. In much argumentation about sexuality, the body and relationships fall apart, or are opposed as natural to social. The key to the difficulty is the implicit equation of 'body' and 'nature'. As long as that equation holds, then the fuller the recognition of the bodily dimension in sexuality—whether in eroticism, violence, male/female bodily difference—the stronger the push towards nativism. The tendency is clear in some feminist argument about sexual violence. Argument that emphasizes the social tends to be bloodless, to lose the sweat and passion. This can be seen in role theory, in semiotics, and in structural analysis.

3 'The Unclean Motion of the Generative Parts'

It is only with a concept of *the body as social* that the problem can be overcome. Such a concept has been worked out in relation to gender (Kessler and McKenna 1978, Connell 1987: 66–88). The very limited biological differences of sex are appropriated by a social process which constructs gender oppositions as taken-for-granted facts of life, naturalizes them, and even transforms the body in pursuit of a social logic. This process is dramatically shown in the social history of fashion (Wilson 1987).

Keat (1986) makes a similar point in showing that Reich and Foucault, far from being polar opposites, in fact share a position on this issue. The relationship of biological to social processes, Keat argues, does not occur at a boundary between 'the body' and 'society'. It is internal to the human body itself. Bodily processes such as muscular tensions, physical attitudes, etc., are already social. Turner's (1984: 190ff) concept of 'body practices' emphasizes the collective and cultural aspect of this (and perhaps over-emphasizes the intentional).

In relation to sexuality this approach will emphasize such issues as the construction of sexual desirability (the social meanings of age, among other things, being important here); the control of fertility (for instance recent feminist work on the social meaning of in vitro fertilization); the social structuring of arousal ('Never the time, the place/And the loved one all together!'); the collective dimension in body self-images and body fantasies (as illustrated by Glassner's (1988) research on the industry that has grown up in the United States around appearance and fitness).

This approach has some disturbing consequences for methodology in the social sciences. The effect of abstraction in research practices, especially in quantification and experimentation, is to eliminate whole, functioning bodies as components of social–scientific knowledge. In terms of research on sexuality, this has the odd and important effect that fucking is treated as an act of cognition. In this sense it is capable of incorporation into language and therefore is able to be reflected on and represented abstractly. It can be studied in the accounts of individuals as an assemblage of sexual events. Inventories of sexual practices such as those retrieved in sexual diary keeping (Davies 1990) provide a striking example of the schematization of sexuality that results. Our argument would suggest the crucial importance of research methods open to an understanding of embodiment, the choreography of sex, the tactics of sensation, the manoeuvres of desire.

Finally, we need to consider the political implications of the theoretical re-focusing being proposed. A driving force in the theoretical work of the 1960s and 1970s was the idea of sexual liberation. This concept combined two ideas: the lifting of social prohibitions on sexual behaviour (as in the journalistic notion of 'permissiveness'), and the dismantling of the power of one social group over another. In the 1970s, in the work of gay activists and theorists influenced by radical readings of Freud (Altman 1972, Mieli 1980), this approached the idea of a general social revolution fuelled by sex as a kind of erotic explosive. It was a considerable comedown from this to the Foucauldian notions of sexuality as an effect of power and of gay sexual identity as a product of 'regulation'. Social framing theories helped the critique of nativist models of deviance, but they did not point towards positive goals for change.

It now seems clear that the prospect of sexual revolution (and gay liberation) became transformed in practice as well as in theory in the developing modern gay communities. It modulated into a pursuit of the self in sex, a claim to sexual rights, exercised in the institutionalized sex-on-premises venues and in a growing sense of gay community. A more conspicuous manifestation was the reclaiming of masculinity by gay men, that colonization of masculine imagery and style, which simultaneously undermined classic masculine pretence. The irony of this colonization was not lost on gay men themselves (Bersani 1988). Gay liberation was not alone during the 1970s and 1980s in this softening of agendas. Segal (1987) traces the internal conflicts in British feminism that led to a shift from the defence of erotic freedom in the face of an essentially nativist emphasis on sexual difference.

3 'The Unclean Motion of the Generative Parts'

The agenda of gay liberation was not completely lost, nor reduced to civil liberties. It remained sufficiently available to challenge the early responses to the HIV epidemic which called for homosexual celibacy, and was able to produce the idea of 'safe sex' as we now know it. Safe sex and later programs which mobilize its erotic and transgressive character (Gordon, unpublished; Dowsett 1990) are examples of the importance of this early recognition of power in sexuality.

A fully social concept of sexuality, of the kind discussed in the previous section, would revive the concept of sexual liberation. But the concept would take a different form from the idea of an erotic explosion. Rather it would have to do with the democratization of the social relationships constituted through sexuality.

As in the earlier argument, homosexuality may play a leading role in this, but for a different reason. It is significant not so much as the site of the severest repression, but as the milieu of the most egalitarian sexual relationships currently available as models in our culture. The high degree of reciprocity in gay men's sexual practice (documented in Connell and Kippax 1990) suggests one path forward.

The need for a revitalized liberation agenda becomes more urgent with regard to the negotiation of safe sex in the face of the HIV epidemic. Part of the success of gay men's responses to sexual behaviour change is, arguably, due to this reciprocity. Kippax, Crawford, Waldby et al. (1990) have argued that HIV/AIDS prevention strategies designed for heterosexuals may not be able to rely on the same negotiation, given the structure of power relations in heterosexuality which disadvantage women. Liberation in sexual relationships is thus not only an expressive demand. It is crucially connected with the struggle for *equality* between social groups.

4
ABSOLUTE SEX? UNPACKING THE SEXUALITY/GENDER RELATIONSHIP

Rosemary Pringle

> And she is simply what man decrees; thus she is called 'the sex', by which is meant that she appears essentially to the male as a sexual being. For him she is sex—absolute sex, no less (de Beauvoir 1953: 16)

Sexuality and gender are conventionally seen as separate but overlapping categories. We are regularly reminded that they are not reducible to each other, and that it is perfectly possible to work with one without necessarily invoking the other. Much has already been done to unravel the normative connections that have been made between the two. Feminists have resisted the definitions of women in exclusively sexual terms while gay theorists have criticized the reading of homosexuality in gender terms—effeminate men and butch women. While it has been important to challenge the crude assumptions about how sexuality and gender interact, a number of conceptual problems remain. These are not solved by simply treating the two as social constructions, as scripts or discourses which to some extent overlap. What they share is a relationship to that ambiguous third term 'sex', which has created problems for any kind of social construction theory. In reconceptualizing gender and sexuality, those other two sides of the triangle, sex and sexuality, and sex and gender are very important.

The categories of sexuality and gender have a schizoid relationship. For much of the time they ignore each other completely, with the result that there is a large literature which treats sexuality as if gender barely exists and another literature on gender that ignores or marginalizes sexuality. Despite this, assumptions are constantly made about their connectedness. Students taking my sexuality course, for example, often assume that an essay on any aspect of 'women's studies' will be relevant to its main themes. This easy translation of sexuality into 'woman' probably derives from the Victorian habit of referring to women as 'the sex'. It is based, of course, on a masculine perspective, and the same is true for the study of sexuality as it has developed since the nineteenth century. Though sexual theorists have treated sexuality itself in a 'unisex' fashion, their definitions of the sexual act (penetration) and of sexual drive (libido) were masculine ones; it was in masculine interests to deny female specificity and to play down issues relating to gender and power.

SEXUAL MODERNISM AND ITS CRITICS

Research on sexuality was part of the modernist tradition as it developed from in the late nineteenth and early twentieth centuries. Sexual modernism represented a self-conscious reaction against what it conceived as Victorian orthodoxy. It perceived itself as progressive in that it regarded sexual experience in positive terms, encouraged the expression of female sexuality and defended the rights of homosexuals and other sexual minorities. 'Sex research' opened up to scientific investigation an area of life previously designated as private and therefore not open to large-scale investigation and public discussion. Feminists have recently argued, however, that although it purported to be objective and scientific it was in fact biased towards the interests of men. Female sexuality was not ignored but, in the work of the 'landmark' theorists, Havelock Ellis, Kinsey et al. and Masters and Johnson, it was defined as either complementary to or the same as male sexuality. It is true that Kinsey gleefully stressed the disjunction between male and female sexuality, with women peaking in their late thirties and men in decline in their early twenties (1948,

1953). But Kinsey was essentially a spokesman for the sexual rights of adolescent males. While he boasted about his objectivity his approach to sexuality is brashly masculine. Sexual experience is defined strictly in terms of orgasms, and orgasms strictly in terms of numbers. He took no note of how they differed from each other in intensity, or in the emotional values associated with them. He justified this on pragmatic grounds as the only objective measurement. While this implied that all orgasms were equal, whatever their source, in fact Kinsey stressed the importance of early sexual experience for successful marriage.

The 1960s brought an era of sexual permissiveness couched in terms of 'sexual revolution'. Perhaps more than at any earlier time sexual theorists ignored gender as a major constituent of sexuality. The similarity between men and women is a prominent theme in Masters and Johnson's *Human Sexual Response* (1966). They claimed to have finally refuted psychoanalytic accounts of sexual difference by showing, once and for all, that male and female sexual responses followed the same physical patterns. Indeed sex was reduced to a set of physical responses, apparently disconnected from psychological, emotional or power dimensions. From this it seemed to follow that women should henceforth have the freedom to behave like men. It was a masculine model which assumed that what was good for men was automatically good for women. The greater availability of abortion and the arrival of the Pill and other forms of birth control were seen as relieving women of their remaining biological disadvantages, and giving them access to 'sex' on the same terms as men.

'Contemporary' sexual theory really begins with the New Left in the 1960s. In contrast to the Old Left, there was a much greater emphasis on sexual and cultural questions, and in particular with explaining how the old working class had been incorporated into monopoly capitalism. The New Left, which developed in Western countries in the 1960s in the context of the student, civil-rights and anti-war movements, identified sex as potentially revolutionary. Its gurus, like Marcuse (1955), Brown (1970) and Reiche (1974) drew on an amalgam of Freud and Marx to provide a sexual

4 Absolute Sex?

dimension to analyses of class oppression. They did accept the periodization of Bachofen, Engels and others of a matriarchal, egalitarian society having given way to patricentric, authoritarian culture, but this was never translated into a gender politics which scrutinized relations between men and women. It was not women who should rise up against patriarchal culture but the working class, the 'enslaved' sons. Like Kinsey, the New Left were effectively speaking up for the sexual rights of young working-class men. Marcuse developed the idea of 'surplus repression' that was directly analogous to 'surplus value'. He argued that working-class sexual deprivation is of enormous significance for the organization of social and economic life. 'Surplus repression' referred to that repression, over and above what was necessary to provide the energy for social existence, which fuelled class domination. In particular, the desexualization of the body, and the confinement of erotic pleasure to the genitals, is a precondition for transforming the body into an instrument of labour. Marcuse criticized the reduction of sexuality to a narrow genitality that was compatible with the harnessing of the body to the exigencies of the capitalist workplace. The goal was thus the re-sexualizing of the whole body and the 'polymorphous perverse' came to be celebrated as both a means and end of revolutionary action.

Confronted with the emergence of a consumer-oriented society in which sexuality seemed anything but repressed, Marcuse later developed the concept of 'repressive desublimation' to explain the shift. He noted that whereas in earlier times restrictions on sexual gratification were necessary for the survival of civilization, in a non-scarcity society this was no longer necessary. Sexuality was now expressed but in ways that integrate it into 'commerce and industry, entertainment and advertising, politics and propaganda' (Brown 1973: 160).

What is perhaps most striking now is that at neither stage did Marcuse pay more than passing attention to gender. Masculinity and femininity were simply the active and passive forms of the same sexual drive (Weeks 1985: 169). At most it could be argued that 'more' surplus repression was extracted from women: the issue was purely a quantitative one. Women were oppressed, not by men, but by the capitalist system. As the following quotation makes clear, Marcuse thought both sexes were oppressed in much the same way:

> ... without ceasing to be an instrument of labour, the body is allowed to exhibit its sexual features in the everyday work world and in work relations ... The sexy office and sales girls, the handsome, virile junior executive and floor worker are highly marketable commodities ... Sex is integrated into work and public relations and is thus made susceptible to (controlled) satisfaction ... Pleasure, thus adjusted, generates submission. (1968: 70–71)

Despite his attention to the socio-cultural, Marcuse had a highly naturalistic conception of the instincts in conflict with reality. While allowing that the expression of sexual instincts varied from one culture to another, he did not locate himself amongst theories that stressed the social construction of sexuality, which were also developing in the 1960s. These theories, which treated gender and sexuality both as social constructions, had more scope for considering the two in relation to each other. The best that can be said is that in his key texts Marcuse ignored gender. Where earlier theorists like Reich (1969) had attacked the patriarchal family, Marcuse, like many in the American New Left, was inclined to romanticize the family as a possible site of resistance against mass culture.

Marcuse's emphasis on polymorphous pleasure seemed to open the doors for women as well as gays and other sexual minorities. But there were problems, for questions of sexuality and power had not been addressed. As Weeks points out, sexuality itself was seen as a critical opponent of power, and the refusal of repression was supposed to be inherently liberating (1985: 168–70). There was no notion of the ways in which men and women, gays and straights were differently placed in relation to sexuality, of the plurality of forms of control, or the constructive modes of the operations of power. Women found 'sexual revolution' damaging insofar as it was a licence for male promiscuity and placed pressure on them to be available without any

4 Absolute Sex?

emotional commitments and without the freedom simply to reverse the roles. As Marge Piercy put it in *The Grand Coolie Damn*: 'A man can bring a woman into an organization by sleeping with her and remove her by ceasing to do so. A man can purge a woman for no other reason than that he has tired of her, knocked her up, or is after someone else' (quoted by Snitow et al. 1983: 20). In the name of 'liberation' heterosexual men were blandly denying their own sexual exploitation of women. Because sexuality was such a big issue in the New Left, it actually created potential for increasing male dominance. The Freudian–Marxist approaches failed to take any account of men's power and, with all their assumptions about 'natural sexuality', failed to acknowledge the specificity and variety of sexualities.

The feminist writings of the early 1970s challenged notions of 'sexual revolution' and pointed instead to men's sexual power. They argued not only that sexuality was male defined but that men's domination was eroticized and that sexual power was the *key* to masculine control of every sphere of life. Far from being a by-product of economic or political power, the specifically sexual was made central. In the most famous statement, Millett (1972) redefined Reich's term 'sexual politics' to refer to power-structured relationships whereby one sex is controlled by the other. Hite (1977) criticized what she called the 'reproductive model' which defined 'the real thing' in terms of penetration, intercourse and male orgasm, with other sexual activity relegated to 'foreplay' and female orgasm optional (527–8). Others went on to criticize the institution of heterosexuality itself. Koedt's 'Myth of the Vaginal Orgasm' (1973) documented the ways in which female sexuality had been structured around men's convenience, denying the physical bases of women's sexual pleasure. It offered a re-evaluation of lesbianism which, far from being an *impoverished* expression of sexuality, could be seen as a viable alternative and even a better one.

The one area where sexual theorists treated gender as central was with reference to homosexuality where a lot of clichéd assumptions were and still are made about the connections between 'gender' and sexual preference (masculine/feminine and active/passive). A homosexual man who favoured 'passive' sexual positions could think of himself as having a feminine temperament, while to espouse a homosexual identity meant to be viewed as a 'gender freak'. Homosexual desire could effectively be denied by being reinterpreted in heterosexual terms as the feminine in one person reaching out to the masculine in another. The association of gay men with femininity and lesbian women with masculinity amounted to a denial of same sex attraction and made heterosexuality conceptually inescapable.

The historical connections need to be researched and explained rather than taken for granted. The distinction between gender identity and sexual orientation is actually quite recent. Marshall (1981) identifies five basic components to sexual identity that are presumed to be in alignment in 'real' men and women. Along with sex, gender identity and gender role these are sexual behaviour (patterns of sexual activity) and sexual meaning—the way in which sexual activity and identity are interpreted and experienced by actors. It has been an important contribution of the gay movement to deconstruct these connections. In reaction to the association between male homosexuality and effeminacy, gay machismo emerged as an apparent celebration of a heightened masculinity. Gay men took on traditionally masculine images—cowboys, police, soldiers, athletes, leathermen and so on, and celebrated them in the context of a promiscuous public-sex clone culture (Humphries 1985; Edwards 1990). It is an open question how far this subverts the dominant culture and how far, as some feminists have argued, it merely reinforces it, but it does demand a conceptual separation of sexuality and gender. This has been followed up by Rubin who, as a spokesperson for sexual minorities, has insisted that in principle gender should not be relevant to practices such as sado-masochism (1979). For Rubin, the feminist insistence on difference is part of an ongoing moralizing about sex by both lesbian and heterosexual women. It can be argued that feminists, despite their protestations, have actually been reluctant to let go of the heterosexual institutions

4 Absolute Sex?

which provide the basis for a whole range of feminist politics.

Butler (1990a, 1990b) has also attacked the heterosexual bias of most modern social theory, stressing the need to free sexual expression from the strait-jacket of binary gender categories. She points out that even in versions of psychoanalysis that claim to be non-essentialist, desire is presumed to function through a gender difference instituted at the symbolic level and is structured in ways that are inevitably heterosexual. She comments:

> Although Rose, Mitchell, and other Lacanian feminists insist that identity is always a tenuous and unstable affair, they nevertheless fix the terms of that instability with respect to a paternal law which is culturally invariant. The result is a narrativized myth of origins in which primary bisexuality is arduously rendered into a melancholic heterosexuality through the inexorable force of the law ... When bisexuality is relieved of its basis in the drive theory, it reduces, finally, to the coincidence of two heterosexual desires, each proceeding from oppositional identifications or dispositions, depending on the theory, so that desire, strictly speaking, can issue only from a male-identification to a female object or from a female-identification to a male object. (1990a: 332–3)

Butler's main concern here is with the ways in which lesbianism is made invisible. In Kristeva's frame of reference, for example, lesbianism can only refer to the prohibited incestuous love between daughter and mother, to be resolved through maternal identification and literally becoming a mother. Yet the category of 'lesbian' can no more be taken as given than that of 'woman'. 'What qualifies as a lesbian?' asks Butler. 'Does anyone know?' (1990b: 127).

Whether dealing with gender or sexual preference, we have to be aware of the contexts in which difference is asserted or denied. Ironically, given the tenacity of the connection between homosexual attraction and gender divergence, 'homosexuality' as a category is still persistently used in a gender-blind way. Though homosexual men and lesbians occupy vastly different worlds they are still lumped together. Remember the early phase of the HIV/AIDS panic when 'homosexuals' were excluded from donating blood.

Lesbians, unless intravenous drug users or having heterosexual intercourse with members of that group, are one of the safest groups in the community. Yet they are still perceived by the general community as only slightly less at risk than gay men.

Feminists and gays have needed to separate sexuality and gender in order to establish the ways in which they have been historically constructed in relation to each other. Despite their efforts, much contemporary writing on sexuality is either gender-blind (Foucault) or fails to take seriously the question of male power (Lacan). Contesting the sexist and heterosexist, phallocentric and logocentric, not to mention ethnocentric, assumptions of post-structuralist thought has become a full-time occupation for many. Yet there is still a conceptual awkwardness of two separate 'variables' which intersect and overlap. There has been much debate about which is the more all-encompassing category, sexuality or gender. This often arranges sexuality and gender according to some kind of base/superstructure model, asking which is more fundamental. In psychoanalytic versions, sexuality is the cloth from which gender is cut; in interactionist terms the sexual can be included among a larger range of gender scripts. Locked into this too is the debate about sameness and difference. Those who see an essential similarity between men and women tend to focus on an undifferentiated sexuality; those who stress difference point to the gendered nature of discourse and argue that equality is impossible until female desire can be represented independently of masculine 'norms'. The lurking difficulty is the series of binary categories (man/woman, same/different, and perhaps sexuality/gender) that continue to close off discussion.

DISCOURSE AND SEX

I want to trace some of the main usages of the terms gender and sexuality, noting what has happened to them in the light of collapse in the faith in grand theories, whether structuralist, Marxist, feminist or all of these. Whether we identify as 'post-structuralists' or not, post-structuralism has

4 Absolute Sex?

had a major impact on how most of us see the world. What we have seen is a move away from explanations that evoke different levels of reality and the relation between them, whether base/superstructure models or not. There is a rejection of the idea that some levels of reality are more fundamental than others; and, while the existence of 'reality' is not denied, there is a substantial agreement that it becomes knowable and meaningful only through discourse.

Since the 1960s social construction theories have become influential and, in some circles, dominant although they have not succeeded in dislodging mainstream literatures in bio-medicine and sexology (Vance 1989). Social construction theories have taken a number of forms, the first of which was symbolic interactionism. Where, for drive theorists, sexual meaning is relatively unproblematic, for interactionists the central task has been to analyse the processes by which sexual meanings are constructed. Rather than taking the sexual as fixed or intrinsic, as both Freudian and empiricist accounts had done, it emphasized the 'meanings' of sexuality. Meanings were perceived as social products, as creations that are formed in and through the defining activities of people as they interact. And it is this complex of ongoing activity that establishes and portrays social structure or organization. Our material worlds have to be interpreted and given sense through a dense web of negotiable symbols which are historically produced. Such meanings are not given and fixed. They are precarious and ambiguous and have to be constantly negotiated and worked at in the ceaseless stream of social interaction.

The most important contributions to theories of sexuality within this framework were Gagnon and Simon's *Sexual Conduct* (1974) and Plummer's *Sexual Stigma* (1975). Gagnon and Simon specifically referred to 'conduct' and not 'behaviour' to indicate that sexual conduct is learnt conduct and can be studied just like any other. It is only because we have invented such a special importance for human sexuality, they argued, that we have also needed to invent special theories to deal with it. Theorizing abut sex has been shaped by the culture which generated it and this has served to structure, indeed 'construct', sexualities. Both Gagnon and Simon and Plummer argued that sexuality should not be seen as a powerful drive but rather as a socially constructed motive; they emphasized the metaphor of the 'sexual script' as a framework for analysing the social construction of sexual meaning; and the need to view sexual development not as something relentlessly unwinding from within but as something constantly shaped through encounters with significant others. Plummer emphasized the wider socio-historical formations which generate the identities which people assume and specifically the importance of stigmatic labelling in creating the separate worlds of sexual deviance.

It was a short step from this to the current emphasis on discourses and practices. Where we now talk about 'discourses' they talked about 'scripts'; and scripts defined both gender roles and sexual situations. But scripts presumed the existence of individual actors who learnt their parts; the question of power was never more than marginal. Discourse theory, on the other hand, allows no pre-existing actors, and concentrates on the ways in which subject positions are produced by the discourse. Discourses relate to wider frameworks of meaning, are inseparable from practices, and frequently have strong institutional bases. Discursive practices routinely produce power and resistance.

For Foucault (1978), discourses on sexuality have become of central importance to the control and regulation of populations. Rather than repressing sexuality, they actively produce it. 'Sexuality' is set up as the key to our identity, and we engage actively with the 'norms' thus created, in order to find our true selves. The sexual discourses identified by Foucault produce gendered figures, but not in any systematic way. The characteristic figures of the hysterical woman and the homosexual man (gendered) are more than counter-balanced by the Malthusian couple and the masturbating child (where gender is ignored or denied—surely it relates to a male child). He is concerned with the multiplicity of positions, including gendered ones, that are produced by discourse, and what this means in terms of power and resistance. But he is not interested in the ways

4 Absolute Sex?

in which discourse itself might be said to be masculine. When he connects sexuality and power he does so in quite orthodox class terms. For example, he criticizes Marcuse, pointing out that if the purpose of sexual repression was a more intensive use of the labour force, one would expect the machinery of repression would have been directed above all at the working class, in particular the young, adult male. Yet the most rigorous techniques were applied by the privileged to themselves. This, he says, suggests the self-affirmation of a dominant class, rather than the enslavement of the working class. The enslavement, in this context, of middle-class women is nowhere discussed. Indeed when such women appear in Foucauldian texts, they are more likely to be in alliance with various parts of the state apparatuses (Donzelot 1979).

Along with other post-structuralists Foucault rejects fixed identities, gendered or otherwise, and emphasizes that we take a variety of positions in a variety of discourses. He also rejects any 'essential' sexuality. Discourses on sexuality do not rest on some sort of physical base that we might call 'sex'; on the contrary, they define what is regarded as 'sex' and what is not. Butler has made a similar point with regard to gender, arguing that it is the apparatuses of gender that actually produce 'sex'. Gender, she says, is 'the discursive/cultural means by which "sexed nature" or "a natural sex" is produced and established as "prediscursive," prior to culture, a politically neutral surface *on which* culture acts' (1990b: 7). This is the most extreme statement of an anti-essentialist position which treats the body as a discursive construction.

The problems with such a position have been outlined by Vance (1989) who confronts us dramatically with this in relation to female circumcision. The most hardened social constructionists are likely to retreat rapidly into essentialism when faced with the unsettling questions raised by the practice of clitoridectomy. Vance suggests that the solution, however, lies not in essentialism 'but in exploring more sensitive and imaginative ways of considering the body' (1989: 26). Discourse theory does not need to argue the 'truth' of one position over another. Instead, each instance of essentialist discourse can be read strategically and contextually (Fuss 1989).

The shift to discourse makes it possible to bypass the old debates about the relation between different levels and structures. Across a range of otherwise incompatible theories, sexuality and gender had been viewed as in some sense superstructural. Whether they referred to roles, scripts, ideologies or representations, they implicitly referred back to some physical, biological, bodily base—known in both cases as 'sex'. Sex referred both to an act and to a category of person, male or female. In Marxist terms this was problematic hence there were attempts to play down the importance of biology and the body. People thus hesitated to use the term 'sex' because it conveyed the dreaded 'essentialism'. Once freed from 'realist' epistemologies, they no longer had to perceive sex or bodies in this way. The body could be read through a variety of discourses, of which biology was only one. Emphasis shifted to the lived body, the body marked by cultural practices, rather than the body as a laboratory object. This renewed interest in the body paved the way for a reconsideration of 'sex' as the suppressed term.

While gender has for a long time attracted the greater theoretical interest, it has recently shown signs of being displaced. Thompson (1989: 23) suggests that, in any case, feminists mostly used the term gender to imply no more than that sex is a social construction and not a purely biological one. 'Sex', which went out fashion after the early 1970s, is, along with bodies, and especially sexed bodies, staging a comeback. Foucault has been criticized for not treating the body as sex-differentiated. Even male writers, both gay and straight, are becoming aware of the implications of sexed bodies.

The trend back to 'sex' is particularly clear in recent feminist work: in MacKinnon's reiteration of men's sexual power, especially in her analysis of pornography (1987); in Pateman's more nuanced account of the 'sexual contract' which guarantees men right of sexual access to women's bodies (1988), and in Allen's recent history of women and crime, *Sex and Secrets* (1990b). Allen declines to include gender in her index and provocatively commences her book as follows:

> Sex has been of central cultural significant in modern Australian history ... Sex is a key dimension of historical subjects. Sex is axiomatic rather than an optional variable. Sex counts.

Pateman stresses that 'men do not exercise power as, or over a "gender" but over embodied women. Men ... exercise power as a sex, and wield sexual power' (1990: 402). Sex is being used here to refer not to biology, but to the importance of bodily difference, where the body itself is perceived as a cultural product: 'Nature, bodies, biology, sex, have always have a social and political meaning'.

This usage is not so different from Millett's in *Sexual Politics* (1972). But Millett was one of the first to get caught up in the sex/gender distinction. In her efforts to understand the sexual meanings of men and women, she drew on the work of Stoller (1968), an analyst who in theorizing transsexualism had made a distinction between sex as a biological component and gender as the social element of sexual difference. Stoller showed that by the age of two or three what he called 'core gender identity' was so strong that it could prevail over biology where the two conflicted. Millett took this as evidence not of the irrelevance of biology but of the importance of complex psychological, cultural and historical factors in creating 'men' and 'women'. But the distinction between the biological and the social was to become more rigid as the 1970s wore on.

GENDER PERSPECTIVES

So far the accent has been on sexuality in its relation to gender. In this section the focus will be on gender and the perspectives on sexuality that emerge when gender is taken as the starting point. Gender has been used in a most confusing variety of ways to refer to the distinctions between at least three different levels: male and female, men and women, masculinity and femininity. Each of these pairs has also been used in a variety of overlapping ways. One person's use of male/female will overlap with another's use of men/women; or again one person will refer to men/women in terms that seem similar to another's use of masculinity/femininity, depending on what kinds of theoretical frameworks they are using. To add to the confusion the French, who have been so influential in these debates, make no distinction between sex and gender and are thus able to fudge the biological and the social or linguistic.

Some psychologists and sociologists initially used gender to mean biological sex, male or female (Chafetz 1974). This was distinguished from 'sex role', which referred to 'a set of behavioral, temperamental, emotional, intellectual and attitudinal characteristics', and for which the appropriate terms were masculine and feminine. Sex and gender were here used interchangeably, and set against 'role' which was regarded as the appropriate conceptual framework for social science.

More commonly, in psychological and sociological writing, gender came to be separated out from 'biological' sex, and used in tandem with 'sex roles'. Bardwick spoke of psychological gender (sexual identity) and physical gender by which she meant male and female biology (1971). She also distinguished between sex role *preference* and adoption and sex role *identity*, which was linked to masculinity and femininity. While it was acknowledged that unconscious processes were relevant, the psychologists made little attempt to theorize them. They were preoccupied with the technical problems of 'measuring' masculinity and femininity, conceived as personality traits. Biological difference was played down, and the emphasis placed on socialization and stereotyping processes. There was in this kind of work very little reference to sexuality, except in so far as a watered-down version of Freud had become a staple of socialization theory (Parsons and Bales 1956). In mainstream theory the child's Oedipal attachment was perceived as an element that could be used productively in the process of ensuring that the child learnt the appropriate sex roles. Feminists took over socialization theory and shore it of any Freudian elements. Their

4 Absolute Sex?

accounts of sex roles largely ignored sexuality except as an aspect of role.

For role theorists, masculinity and femininity were sets of empirically existing characteristics. According to psychologists like Bem (1974), it was possible and desirable to score highly on both. For a time 'androgyny' looked like the answer to inequalities between men and women, and gays and straights. This approach ruled out any analysis of power relations by reducing gender difference to sets of personality traits and proposing to blend them. It ignored the fact that masculinity and femininity are produced in opposition to each other. As Raymond put it, 'the language and imagery of androgyny is the language of dominance and servitude combined. One would not put master and slave ... together to define a free person' (1979: 161). The theory did not explain why the masculine traits were more highly valued; nor why androgyny seemed more acceptable for men than for women; nor the different meanings that, say, masculinity had in relation to male and female bodies. In a world of androgynous men and women, it looked as if men would still exercise power over women. Androgyny was also proposed as a 'solution' to homosexuality. Yet homosexuals did not necessarily want to become androgynously bisexual. Whether you went to bed with a man or a woman continued to matter!

The separation of sex and gender was important in the early days of the women's movement because it served to make clear that all kinds of roles and behaviours did not automatically arise from the 'facts' of sexual difference. But it is now under attack for treating the relation between the two as arbitrary and for isolating gender characteristics from lived experience. I heard a psychology lecturer recently describing research on changes in sex-typing at different stages of the life cycle. A young married woman, childless, in the full-time workforce and preoccupied with her career, could thus be said to be displaying a high degree of masculinity. The students looked very uncomfortable at this. Perhaps it represented an outdated version of masculinity and femininity. More to the point, it seemed to offend their sense of themselves as men and women, and to have sexual overtones that they found threatening. The distinction between sex and gender was of course made precisely to challenge this conflation of the biological and the social, to indicate that traits and abilities did not have to flow on in any inevitable way from biology. In this case it did not work. Gender, used in this way, strikes no chords with their lived experience or subjectivity. Why? Partly because the binary identities man/woman are so strong that anything that is dissonant with them is thrown off. Whereas a man might be able to incorporate femininity without his manhood being threatened, a 'masculine' woman is censured. While theoretically a sex/gender distinction is helpful, politically it is of limited use.

In a brilliant study of *Gender and Genius* (1989), Battersby casts further light on women's predicament in relation to gender. She demonstrates very clearly that what is downgraded in our culture is not femininity but femaleness. For the romantic tradition, as it developed from the late eighteenth century, it was not reason but sensibility and creativity that made 'man' different from the animals. The genius combined masculine 'virility' with feminine characteristics such as emotion, intuition and imagination, thus transcending his biology. But women could not achieve genius. In the new rhetoric of exclusion, biological femaleness merely mimicked the psychological femininity of true genius (1989: 2–3). Weininger's book *Sex and Character*, which was influential at the turn of the century, popularized the idea that the 'perfect male includes within himself the female. The perfect female is, however, always utterly female' (Battersby 1989: 113). Jungian psychology further reinforced this:

> Just as a man brings forth his work as a complete creation out of his inner feminine nature, so the inner masculine side of a woman brings forth creative seeds which have the power to fertilize the feminine side *of the man* (Jung, as quoted by Battersby 1989: 7)

Even though Jung allowed women a 'masculine' side, it was restricted to influencing male creative power. While the sex/gender distinction was a brave attempt to free women

4 Absolute Sex?

from the destiny of biology, it failed to engage with these powerful cultural traditions or the extent to which female persons, regardless of their 'gender attributes' were regarded as inferior.

Gender identity

A third approach has focused on core gender identity. Although the language of masculinity and femininity remains, in this discourse it takes on a different set of meanings, referring to the process of being and becoming 'men' and 'women'. The concern here is with deeper levels of subjectivity, with the fundamental identities of men or women rather than with psychological traits, roles or behaviours into which we are socialized. For psychoanalytic theory, identity is constructed in the context of conflict, repression and struggle. Socialization is not an easy, gentle process. It is associated with pain and fear, the passionate intensity of thwarted desire and the threats to bodily integrity that are implied in the Oedipal and castration complexes. In Freud's terms the boy has to give up his early identification with his mother and identify with his father. Masculinity involves a repression of the feminine, and an exaggeration of toughness and autonomy, which is achieved at the price of despising women. Girls, on the other hand, experience themselves as 'lacking', and learn that women lack social power, except by making themselves attractive to men. One thinks of Mitchell's account (1974) of 'the making of a lady' and 'the marks of womanhood', as she draws on Freud to provide an account of female sexuality under patriarchy.

Gender and sexuality are here intimately connected, for gender is actually constructed through the whole Oedipal process. It certainly cannot be said that psychoanalytic theories ignore the body. Far from treating the human body as a mere biological specimen, they recognize that it is always lived in culture; that understandings of its workings are themselves cultural productions. But feminists have persistently pointed to the problems about how the body is perceived, that the treatment of the female body is that of an imperfect male, and the failure to see two different kinds of body.

Sexual difference

A fourth position, which I shall call *sexual difference*, straddles American cultural feminism and French critiques of 'phallocentricity', notably those of Irigaray (1985) and Cixous (1980). Dominant in the 1980s, 'difference' involved the assertion and celebration of women's autonomy. Its American advocates have drawn heavily on object relations theory as originally developed by Chodorow, Gilligan and others to emphasize women's fundamentally different sense of self. The relational self (as distinct from the bounded male self) they argue, enables women to be more empathetic, caring and nurturant, and to live in harmony with their environment rather than dominate it. Accused of being 'essentialist', dismissed as being 'cultural' as opposed to 'political' feminists by those who adhered to older models of politics, they could be interpreted as strategically engaged with a masculinity which hides itself as gender-neutral.

This is more explicit with the French 'difference' theorists, who have not taken a separatist or a standpoint position. They have been particularly concerned with debating Lacanian psychoanalysis and with the problem of the feminine being unsymbolized. In regarding the male as the reference point, the female is treated either as the same (not existing separately), or as lacking and hence different from/complementary to the male. The feminine is thus unrepresented or made unrepresentable. Freud describes the girl as initially a 'little man', her clitoris a small version of the penis, her libido masculine. So, in the first instance, she is the same as the boy. She is then confronted with her castration, her 'lack'. No longer is she an inferior version of 'the same' but, worse, she must accept that she is incapable of ever becoming 'the same'. Again, the male is the norm against which she is measured and found wanting. Finally, in the resolution stage, when she gives up her active, clitoral sexuality and turns to men, her position becomes complementary to the man's (Irigaray 1985). In contrast to

4 Absolute Sex?

de Beauvoir, for whom women are designated as the Other, Irigaray argues that both subject and Other are masculine symbols which exclude the feminine. Her work therefore provides a starting point for a criticism of hegemonic representations.

Sexual difference theories reject the term 'gender' in so far as it refers to mental characteristics and plays down the importance of bodily difference. Where these theories mention 'gender' at all it is to insist that degendering amounts to the privileging of the male in the name of gender neutrality. They have criticized a feminist politics based on the abolition of gender as naive and called for alternative strategies which acknowledge the ongoing complexities of differences between men and women. The contribution of women like Irigaray (1985), Rich (1979) and Daly (1978), disparate though they are, has been to attempt to develop a language of female sexuality and female pleasure that does not derive from the masculine. While men have for centuries appropriated the 'feminine' it is the 'female', they argue, that needs to be represented and valued.

Gender and social structure

Difference theory has not been without its critics. Prominent among them is an American historian, who has expressed concern that a difference track will simply mean a withdrawal from any engagement with questions of power (Gordon 1986). She reminds us that 'one main reason women do not, did not, keep to a separate track is, of course the institution of heterosexuality. Institutionalized heterosexuality simultaneously helps to create gender and thus difference, and set limits on that difference' (1986: 27–8). In recent work, historians and sociologists have shifted away from questions about gender and individual subjectivity to focus on gender as social processes and signifying practices. 'Social' is being used here not in contrast to the biological but in contrast to the 'individual'. Connell (1987), Matthews (1984), and Hearn et al. (1989) talk about gender orders, gender regimes, the practices of gender. The historical construction of gender at the level of social organizations is important here. Connell comments that 'there are gender phenomena of major importance which simply cannot be grasped as properties of individuals, however much properties of individuals are implicated in them' (1987: 139). Gender is understood as a set of social practices and a system of cultural meanings.

Feminists have also expanded on discourse theory to show how gender-differentiated meanings and positions are made available to men and women. Hollway (1984), for example, shows that heterosexual relations are a primary site where gender difference is produced; but heterosexual practices signify differently for men and women and may be read through different discourses. De Lauretis has argued the importance of retaining notions of identity, albeit constantly shifting ones. Subjectivity is constructed through a continuous process of interaction with the practices, discourses and institutions that make sense of the world; at the moment of being created women are also creating what they are and changing the ways in which discourses are applied. She thus gives agency to the subject while at the same time placing her within particular discursive formations (1986). De Lauretis uses the term 'technologies of gender' (1989a) to go beyond the limits of sexual difference theory. She takes her title directly from Foucault's theory of sexuality as a 'technology of sex' (1978), criticizing the latter for not taking into account the conflicting investments of men and women in the discourses and practices of sexuality. Gender is a product of social technologies (such as cinema), of institutionalized discourses and critical practices, as well as the practices of daily life. It is the representation of a relation, that of belonging to a category or group. She points out that a 'child' is treated as neutral. Though it has sex from 'nature' it has to be signified as a boy or a girl before it acquires a gender. Social relations are thus predicated on a rigid opposition of two biological sexes.

De Lauretis stresses signifying practices, arguing that to focus on 'sexual difference' is ultimately to be trapped within the dichotomies of Western patriarchy. Nevertheless she has consistently defended difference theorists against charges of essentialism (1989b). She defines women in a nominalist sense rather than a metaphysical one and stresses the importance of creating new discursive spaces for women. Radical feminists have, she suggests, contributed more to this process than come-lately post-structuralists. It is one thing to accept the post-structuralist displacement of the unitary subject and another to deny the gendered nature of discourse. The last thing feminism needs is the setting up of a new binary opposition between 'cultural' and 'post-structural' feminism, or between essentialism and anti-essentialism, just at the point when it is becoming possible to go beyond these either/ors. If it shows anything, deconstruction theory shows the impossibility of ever completely escaping from 'essentialism', since we necessarily use categories of some kind. Though very different in style, Butler (1990b) makes similar points. Arguing that both 'sex' and 'gender coherence' are regulatory fictions, she casts around for ways to subvert both. This involves not denying any sense of identity (an impossibility) but embracing multiple discordant identities as in drag, lesbian butch-femme or overt hemaphrodism, and revelling in the 'gender trouble' thus created.

THE POLITICS OF RESEARCH

What are the research implications of the above account of sexuality and gender? I think we need to study both signifying practices and actual behaviours; and to link them in such a way as to begin to close that huge gap between quantitative studies of sexual behaviour, and psychoanalytic and discursive approaches. I confess that part of me (the voyeur perhaps) would love to see an Australian Kinsey. I can recall submitting a paper on sexuality and consumption to the *Australian and New Zealand Journal of Sociology* (Game and Pringle 1979), which drew on Freud's *Three Essays on Sexuality* to analyse the apparent opening up of the 'acceptable' range of sexual aims, objects and practices with the expansion of consumer capitalism, and the editors kept sending it back and asking, where's your evidence? And there was indeed little evidence of 'sexual conduct' to supplement and support the interpretation of advertising and mass media that we wanted to develop.

But there is not much point in merely repeating Kinsey, or even updating it with more sophisticated sampling or data-collecting techniques. It would ideally be a study that was sensitive to the theoretical advances of the last twenty years in the areas of sexuality and gender. It would need to be more probing about the power relations generated in sexual practices, and to be very gender specific. There is no point, for example, in discussing marital conflict over the introduction of oral sex, as Rubin (1976) does, if you don't specify upon what sort of body the sex is being practised. We need to be aware that heterosexual practices may be read through entirely different discourses by men and women. Alongside the large-scale survey, we need qualitative work in the areas of fantasy and consumption (what, for example, do people actually *do* with pornography?), and more emphasis, I think, on power and pleasure. Male power operates much more effectively when women consent to it and find pleasure therein. While I agree with MacKinnon (1987) on the importance of men's sexual power, I do not see this power as monolithic. Feminists have written surprisingly little about men's sexual pleasure and yet a transformative politics cannot be based on a 'sack-cloth and ashes' approach. As the HIV/AIDS 'safe sex' campaign has well understood, changes in behaviour are more likely to happen if old pleasures are not simply given up but exchanged for new ones.

It is also important to broaden the definition of sexuality to get it away from its almost exclusive focus on private life and/or leisure activity and to look at workplaces and organizational cultures. Hearn and Parkin (1987), Hearn et al. (1989), Game and Pringle (1983), Cockburn (1983) and others have begun to chart this area. My work on secretaries (Pringle 1988) was specifically concerned to explore the centrality of sexuality to the organization of power at work. Far from being marginal or trivial, sexuality structures occupational identities and workplace relationships. It is impossible to answer the question 'what is a secretary?' without reference to sexual and cultural definitions; and the boss–

4 Absolute Sex?

secretary relationship has to be negotiated in the context of prevailing discourses that construct it as a 'master–slave relationship' or alternatively a mother/nanny keeping in order a naughty or chaotic little boy. Both of these play on subliminal sexual fantasies of the sort that are the stock in trade of pornography. While secretaries may try to claim alternative identities as professionals, and most boss–secretary pairs claim to work as a 'team', it does not usually take long for the presence of the other (sexual) discourses to become apparent. While this might be easiest to observe in the boss–secretary relationship, one of the most sexualized of all workplace relationships, it is not, I argue, restricted to it. Far from being an anachronism, the boss–secretary relationship is 'the most visible aspect of a pattern of domination based on desire and sexuality' (1988: 84). While it is the sexuality of the secretary that receives attention, it is there for the consumption of bosses and other *men*, including working-class men who may have no direct dealings with secretaries but who fantasize about office life.

Along similar lines Gutek (1989: 62–3) has pointed out the quite extraordinary extent to which *men's* sexual behaviour at work goes unnoticed. Even though it is generally assumed that men are more sexually active than women, the cluster of characteristics associated with masculinity do not include a sexual component. Men are seen as rational, analytic, assertive and competitive, but not as sexual beings. Women, on the other hand, are seen in almost exclusively sexual terms and it is they who are assumed to 'use' their sexuality at work. Ironically, men appear to use sexuality more than women and in diverse ways. Even when a man goes so far as to say (as one in Gutek's study did) that he encourages sexual overtures from women by unzipping his pants at work, he may escape being viewed as sexual or as more interested in sex than work. Playboys and harassers go largely unnoticed because 'organizational man', goal-oriented, rational, competitive, is not perceived in explicitly sexual terms. Male sexuality blends in with the aims of the organization, while female sexuality distracts men from their work and is viewed as detrimental to the organization. This echoes what I have already said about the importance of showing up male sexuality where it is hidden behind supposed gender neutrality.

The return to 'sex' in feminist and gay research should not be interpreted as a return to essentialism, unless it is, in Braidotti's words, 'essentialism with a difference' (1989: 100). Sex and sexuality are materially connected to bodily experience but this does not mean that there is 'a' single and identifiable male or female sexuality. Bodies have a meaning only to the extent that they are already situated within discourse. While not denying that the 'real' world has an objective existence, contemporary theorists largely take for granted that we make sense of the world through discourse. Identities, whether as sexed, sexual or gendered, are not pre-given. They have to be constructed, articulated and maintained; they do this using the discursive frameworks available to the time and culture. What will be discovered then is the social meanings and significance that have been attached to different expressions of sexuality in men and women. This analysis challenges the idea of an essential sexual instinct waiting to be uncovered, or freed from repression.

In talking about sexuality it is important to avoid the slide from the sexed bodies of women and men to femininity and masculinity referring to ideas, attitudes and consciousness divorced from biological sex. There are long cultural traditions in which men are not only permitted femininity but are said to use it creatively in a way that women cannot (Battersby 1989). Not surprisingly, feminists joke about the 'new, sensitive man' who, yet again, has appropriated feminine traits. Women (except perhaps as tomboys) do not score many points as masculine or androgynous beings. Feminists therefore have concentrated their attention on the categories female/women while male 'progressives' have mostly concerned themselves with 'masculinity'. This emphasis on masculinity rather than men or male sexuality as the target of programs of social change risks neutralizing both sexual difference and sexual politics. The problem, as Gatens observed, is not masculine gender socialization but the valorization of the male (1983: 154). Associated with the valorization of the male is the process of universaliz-

4 Absolute Sex?

ation, in which female sexuality has been subsumed and devalued beneath an overarching social construction of a genderless sexuality, predicated on an unacknowledged maleness.

Feminists have begun to identify the strategies by which masculine discourses have historically valorized and universalized male bodily experience. As de Beauvoir put it, 'the fact of being a man is no peculiarity. A man is in the right in being a man; it is the woman who is in the wrong' (1953: 15). Instead of exposing their own sex to public scrutiny, men typically invest other groups with sexuality. Only at the margins of regulation is heterosexual masculinity made problematical: the more extreme child molesters and rapists, the most visible pimps and brothel-keepers. Beyond that sexuality tends to be regarded as a problem for women and gays, but not for straight men. Only a minority have begun to talk about the day-to-day practices of masculinity. In relation to HIV/AIDS, it seems that it is not 'people' but heterosexual men who are refusing to adopt safe sex practices. Yet the attention is focused on 'at risk' groups, while the source of the risk remain invisible in the discourse.

It is no longer a matter of which terms best describe the 'reality' of sexual difference. Rather it is a matter of the tactical and strategic advantages each display. Feminist theory is currently keeping a fine balance between full-scale embrace of post-structuralism and insistence on the importance of sexual difference. Are the differences between women and men greater than the differences within each category? Given the emphasis on fragmentation and internal difference, the gender categories do not look very stable. The fragmented subject is potentially subversive of any view which asserts a central organizing principle. For this reason Braidotti stresses the need to assert 'the specificity of the lived, female bodily experience, the refusal to disembody sexual difference into a new allegedly postmodern anti-essentialist subject, and the will to re-connect the whole debate on difference to the bodily existence and experience of women' (1989: 91). Without some such notion, all that is specific to feminism will be lost.

5

SEXUALITY AND THE STATE IN TIME OF EPIDEMIC

J. A. Ballard

In November 1984, in the midst of a Federal election campaign, the Queensland Government announced that three babies had died following transfusions of blood from a gay donor carrying the human immunodeficiency virus (HIV). Blood, death and sex are a heady combination in modern Western culture and the Australian media, having already engaged in two bouts of panic over AIDS, threw themselves into a frenzy. Ian Sinclair, then leader of the National Party, obliged them with a declaration that, 'If it wasn't for the promotion of homosexuality as a norm by Labor, I am quite confident that the deaths of these three poor babies would not have occurred' (*Australian*, 17 November 1984). Sexuality had come to stay on the Australian public agenda.

In the absence of an answer to AIDS from medical science, the response of the Commonwealth Minister for Health, Neal Blewett, was one of consultation and education. This meant the funding of explicit messages on sexual practices issued by AIDS Councils established within gay communities. It also meant the incorporation into policy advisory councils of representatives from gay and sex-worker communities previously recognized primarily as subjects for criminal prosecution. Support for community-based education programs put Australia two years ahead of most other Western countries, where HIV/AIDS was not firmly established on the public policy agenda until late in

5 Sexuality and the State in Time of Epidemic

1986, when medical science acknowledged that heterosexual transmission of HIV presented a threat to the 'general population'.

In this paper I consider the implications of Australia's broadly liberal, consultative, public policy response to a new sexually transmitted disease for an understanding of the interaction of the state and sexuality. I begin by surveying recent theories concerning the role of the state in shaping the discourses of sexuality, and then examine the history of the state and homosexuality, before turning to the radical impact of HIV/AIDS on the interaction of the state and sexualities.

THEORIZING THE STATE AND SEXUALITY

Two substantial literatures overlap in their discussion of the state and sexuality. The first, comprising feminist theorizing of the patriarchal state, is primarily focused on gender relations, with relatively little discussion on the specific interaction of the state with sexuality. Much is written about abortion, contraception, prostitution, child sexual abuse, rape, sexual harassment and pornography, often revealing the assumptions concerning sexuality which underlie state intervention on these issues. There is also exploration of more subtle state intervention through a wide range of law and public policy concerning the family, marriage, divorce, child care and such matters as with whom a single parent may cohabit without incurring penalties.

There has been no attempt as yet to tease out the implications of state action for the construction of sexuality underlying these policy areas, and the few attempts to develop a specifically feminist theory of the patriarchal state are surprisingly opaque on sexuality. MacKinnon's recent book *Toward a Feminist Theory of the State* (1989), the first substantial attempt, portrays sexuality simply as a category of violence, and so has disappointingly little to say about specific modes of state action or the shaping of sexuality. Allen, on the other hand, in her essay, 'Does Feminism Need a Theory of "the State"?' (1990a), would deny that the state is a useful concept for feminist analysis, precisely because it aggregates situations which, she argues, can be understood only in their historical specificity.

The other literature of interest here is that which stems from Foucault's (1978) analysis of the history of sexuality. His concern is with the regulation and control of sexuality in the modern period through public discourses, starting with the concept of a population policy in the eighteenth century as complement to the rise of the state and its displacement of the church. These discourses become more powerful with the growth in the nineteenth century of institutions and disciplines which attempted to regulate the human body, particularly those of medicine, psychiatry and law. They focus on the definition and production of normality through techniques of surveillance and control—not in the interest of repression, but that of productivity. The concept of sexuality is itself a product of these discourses of control, one which, Foucault argues, was an aspect of bourgeois self-definition against working-class immorality and aristocratic decadence.

The evolution of state regulation of sexuality has been tracked by Weeks (1981b) for Britain, Kinsman (1987) for Canada and Freedman and D'Emilio (1988) for the United States, but there is no equivalent study of Australia. All of these studies accord with Foucault in showing the development by law and medicine of 'a body understood not as a "thing" to be scientifically described but as a site for the construction of identities that facilitate the functioning of existing structures of power and authority'. For example, Foucault showed 'how medicine helped to create a code that identifies various "sexual perversions" ... [enforcing] a garrulousness about sex that allows for the monitoring of conduct in a society increasingly interested in having conduct measured, predicted, and regulated, rather than a repression or silencing' (Shapiro 1987: 364).

It is not surprising, then, that it is the proscribed forms of 'deviant' sexuality—homosexuality and prostitution—that have lent themselves to broad theorizing about the shaping force of state regulation and categorization. The variety of discourses of control over women's bodies are so diverse that it is difficult, and probably misleading, to con-

5 Sexuality and the State in Time of Epidemic

ceptualize them in general. The discourses through which masculine heterosexuality is codified are much more indirect, for example, through schools and sports and pornography (see, for example, Morgan 1990). The state is less directly implicated, except through the proscription of deviancy, the limitations on adultery and penalties for rape, and such peripheral reinforcements as collusion in the provision of prostitution for troops during 'rest and recreation'. Pateman (1988) argues that the social contract which provided both the liberal state and citizenship with their theoretical underpinnings excluded controls over male sexuality.

The first serious attempt to map fully the terrain of the state in relation to both gender and sexuality is a recent long essay by Connell (1990). Connell is exceptional in drawing on a wide range of feminist and gay studies to produce a complex set of propositions about the patriarchal state as the central institutionalization of gendered power. He sees sexuality as 'part of the domain of human practice organized [in part] by gender relations, and "sexual politics" [as] the contestation of issues of sexuality by the social interests constituted within gender relations' (1990: 509). In other words, he sees the social construction of gender as prior to the constitution of sexuality.

Much of what Connell has to say about the state and gender refers as well to sexuality, but he marks out two areas in which the modern state is specifically relevant to sexuality. One of these concerns regulation, the other the generation of sexual order through the legislative production of the categories of 'prostitute' and 'homosexual', 'transforming what had been a much more fluid play of sexuality into a clearly flagged social barrier'. The case of marriage is similar, in translation from a 'precipitate of kinship rules, local custom and religion ... [to] ... a product of contract as defined and regulated by the state' (1990: 530). Connell is concerned to emphasize capacity for change, and he examines not only the mobilization of women and gay men in response to state discourse and action, but also crisis tendencies in the legitimation of patriarchy, such as the difficulty of retaining intact the separation of public and private on which the liberal patriarchal state is predicated.

Connell comments on the need to maintain a complex view of the state as both process and institutional apparatus, with various levels and sectors of state action producing inevitably conflicting rationalities. Through its power to define and discriminate the legal from the illegal, the encouraged from the discouraged, the state is a major contributor to and enforcer of the categorization of sexuality. This is not simply a matter of the sanctions of criminal law, but also of a vast array of social policy, ranging from policies on population and immigration to those on sex education and access to health and insurance services. Even the medical profession, in so far as it acts within a licensed monopoly of power to define the healthy, the ill and the certifiable, the normal and the deviant, cannot be excluded. There is no single controlling logic, no single discourse, no necessary consistency among these fields of policy, nor among those who interpret and administer a given law or policy. Yet I disagree with Allen and others who argue that no increase in understanding derives from theorizing the state. Without it, we overlook the cumulative effect—greater than the sum of its parts—of discourse and practice by many different agencies.

To focus on the shaping impact of the state is not to suggest that the state is determinative, for it too is shaped by discourse and practice and it incorporates discourses of sexuality developed initially by the church and later by medicine and psychology. Each of these continues to act directly on sexuality, as do folk and community discourses. None the less, the state has a prominent role both through law, which reifies dominant social values by their enforcement through the coercive apparatus of the state, and through the services and controls of the welfare state. The modes of state influence lie first, in labelling categories; second, in explicitly and implicitly encouraging or discouraging identities and behaviour; and third, in effectively institutionalizing various forms of discourse and practice. All of these relate not only to shaping sexuality, but also to the shaping of other identities and there is a variety of

5 Sexuality and the State in Time of Epidemic

theoretical and empirical literatures which explore this—for instance, Minow (1990) on the operation of the law through differentiation, Schaffer on the impact of structures of access to services on those seeking access (for example, Schaffer and Lamb 1974) and Ballard (1987) on the shaping of ethnicity by colonial administration.

As for theorizing sexuality, there are significant problems arising from the pervasiveness of the dominant Western Christian ideology organized around reproductive sexuality within marriage. While other social institutions have had their claims to universality and a basis in 'nature' undermined by comparative and historical analysis, exposing their dependence on specific cultural contexts, '[g]ender and sexuality have been the very last domains to have their natural, biologized status called into question' (Vance 1989: 14). Only since the late 1960s, and particularly since the publication of Foucault's work on the history of sexuality, has sexuality been examined in terms of its social construction (Weeks 1990: 34–7).

The categorizing of sexuality in the modern West is determined primarily in terms of whom you have sex with and what you do. Much of Foucault's insight stems from his study of ancient Greece where, for the citizen, these did not matter so much as whether one was master or slave of one's passions. Anthropologists are also aware of very different regimes of sexual morality in non-Western societies, but this is a subject on which, perhaps because of the extent to which sexual ideology is hegemonic and unexamined, we find it remarkably difficult to shed our ethnocentrism.

THE ROLE OF THE STATE IN CONSTRUCTING HOMOSEXUALITY

In the past fifteen years there has been published a substantial body of research on the historical construction of the modern homosexual, much of it influenced by Foucault's analysis (see especially Weeks 1981a; Duberman et al. 1989; Altman et al. 1989; Halperin 1990; Stein 1990; and Weeks 1990). The earliest of this work (McIntosh 1968) antedated Foucault and stemmed from the debate over law reform in Britain (McIntosh 1981).

The codification of excluded practices and groups has a long and honourable tradition in Western Christianity, most notably in the abominations of Leviticus and in Aquinas's influential categorization of vice against nature: masturbation, bestiality, coitus in an unnatural position and copulation with an undue sex. When Henry VIII ended the jurisdiction of ecclesiastical courts, buggery became a state offence in 1533, and Blackstone's eighteenth-century codification of the laws replaced Leviticus and Aquinas as the modern reference for English courts to unmentionable, even unnameable, vices. By contrast, during the French Revolution the Constituent Assembly decriminalized homosexual acts between consenting adults and the Code Napoléon maintained this position for France and much of Europe, though Prussia and the German Empire imposed exceptionally harsh penalties.

While homosexual behaviour can be found in all societies, though with very different cultural meanings, the emergence of 'the homosexual' as a cultural construct can be traced to the late seventeenth and early eighteenth centuries in urban centres of north-west Europe (Trumbach 1989a, 1989b) and also linked with the rise of capitalism (D'Emilio 1983). Medical and psychiatric discourses provided the concept and labels of homosexuality and inversion from the 1860s, but for Britain it was the Labouchere amendment to the *Criminal Law Amendment Act 1885*, criminalizing 'gross indecency' between men, which institutionalized the change from sodomy as an aberrant act to the homosexual as a species of individual. The application of this law in the trial of Oscar Wilde ten years later then drew a very sharp and public differentiation between the permissible and the forbidden and helped shape discourse in the English-speaking world on the ordering of homosexuality for over half a century (see Weeks 1981b: 96–117).

Weeks notes that major enactments affecting male homosexuality in Britain from the 1880s on were primarily concerned with female prostitution and he comments that

5 Sexuality and the State in Time of Epidemic

'[w]hat was at stake was on the one hand the uncontrolled lusts of certain types of men, and on the other the necessary sanctity of the sexual bond within marriage' (1981b: 106). It seems possible too that the linkage results from the construction of the prostitute as the 'other' for virtuous women, and of the newly identified homosexual as the counter-image for gentlemen; since both were constructed within male-dominated discourses the total omission of the lesbian from the purview of the law is not surprising.

In 1954, following a period of moral panic over the increasing visibility of prominent homosexuals (in the Burgess–Maclean case and the Montagu–Wildeblood trial) and of street-walking prostitutes, a Committee on Homosexual Offences and Prostitution was appointed, chaired by Lord Wolfenden. In line with proposals from within the Church of England the Wolfenden Committee recommended a restructuring of the law, decriminalizing private behaviour but strengthening penalties for public display. The proposals on prostitution were rushed into law, driving prostitution off the streets and impelling its reorganization through commercial agencies and call-girl rackets. The proposals on homosexuality, on the other hand, took a decade for enactment in the *Sexual Offences Act 1967*. They represented not so much an acceptance of homosexuality as a change in official definition: the 1967 act, which left the public/private distinction undefined, triggered a substantial increase in police prosecution for public indecency, and the language of the courts made clear the continuing outcast status of the homosexual (Moran 1989).

The Wolfenden Committee set out a new 'moral taxonomy' (Weeks 1981b: 244) for the period of reform and 'permissiveness' of the 1960s, in which other issues bearing on sexuality—family planning, abortion, and divorce—were radically redefined in Britain. In a brilliant essay on this 'legislation of consent' Hall argues that the Wolfenden Committee separated legal and moral practice, staking out 'a new relation between the two modes of moral regulation—the modalities of legal compulsion and of self-regulation' (1980: 11–12). 'The field of moral conduct was not dismantled or overthrown, but it was dislocated, rearranged, it received a new inflection. The pivot of this re-articulation was the public/private distinction', with public morality represented by 'right-thinking man' and private morality by 'economic man' seeking an exchange of equivalents. This, Hall argues, constituted a more privatized and person-focused basis for regulation (1980: 19).

On the impact of these changes, Mort concluded, '[w]e should be aware that politically we continue to occupy a space which is very much formed in the aftermath of Wolfenden. In terms both of the lived relations within the gay community, and in the formation of the identities of gay men, we are very heavily structured by the dual strategies of regulation and tolerance which govern homosexuality in the Wolfenden Report' (1980: 37). It would be impossible to make a comparable sweeping claim about the impact of any state-sanctioned redefinition of the sexuality of women, though the legislation of the 1960s substantially enlarged the area of women's consent on sexual issues.

Australian law on homosexuality generally followed British precedent up to the 1960s, and Australian law reform on homosexuality in the 1970s and 1980s followed the logic of Wolfenden. Within the framework of human rights the issue of homosexual law reform was first raised by the Humanist Society at the Australian National University in response to a prosecution following police entrapment in 1968, a year after the passage of the *Criminal Offences Act* in the United Kingdom. The impetus for adoption of the Wolfenden formula was taken up by the Whitlam government, particularly by Bill Hayden, and the first reform legislation was adopted in South Australia in 1973, while the last was passed in Queensland in 1990 and rejected in Tasmania in 1991. By the early 1970s there was substantial mobilization among the first openly gay groups to press for law reform in each of the states, but public debate on the issue in Australia has generally been confined to Parliaments and has never raised the level of public consciousness achieved by the extended and highly contested campaign for decriminalization in New Zealand during 1985–86.

5 Sexuality and the State in Time of Epidemic

None the less, public assertion and self-definition of gay and lesbian identities in Australia (see Thompson 1985, Wotherspoon 1991), as in Britain and the United States, provided the first mobilized opposition to discourses imposed by the state and other authorities. Altman (1982: 108–45) suggests, in a study of the interaction of the gay movement and politics, that much political mobilization on grounds of sexuality has taken place in reaction to persecution by state agencies or to oppressive legislation. Campaigns were not limited to the reform of criminal law, but also to the extension of anti-discrimination legislation to gay and lesbian rights. In Australia, only New South Wales and South Australia legislated against discrimination on grounds of sexual preference, and the New South Wales Anti-Discrimination Board was the only state agency in the pre-HIV/AIDS period taking a strong interest in the protection of gay rights.

THE IMPACT OF HIV/AIDS

The urgent need for a state response to HIV/AIDS has placed sexuality much more firmly and explicitly on the public agenda than on any previous occasion. The link between the risk of disease and the development of discourse on sexuality is not new; the arrival of syphilis in Europe in the fifteenth and sixteenth centuries led to Puritan strictures on sexuality (Andreski 1989), and the availability of antibiotics and the Pill were preconditions for the open flowering of sexualities in the 1960s. But the logic of HIV transmission, once understood, has required an unprecedented articulation of public discourse on sexuality and an unprecedented range of explicit state interventions. On one hand, it has greatly reinforced the demand to know about sexual behaviour and to control it. On the other, recognition of the need to rely on self-regulation has provided incentive for a comprehensive review of state activities impinging on sexuality.

Like other countries, Australia faced a choice of strategies for responding to HIV/AIDS. All Western governments had developed by early in this century a battery of compulsory public-health controls for epidemics and sexually transmitted diseases: surveillance, testing, notification, contact tracing and isolation. Each of these is central and legal in its operation and is intended to identify and categorize bodies on the basis of perceived risks. History has shown them to have been applied primarily to minority groups and prostitutes, seen as 'others' who carry risks to 'the general population'.

Hence the crude labelling of 'risk groups' rather than risk activities. In the case of AIDS, it was first recognized and labelled primarily through its incidence among gay men, and delay in admitting the possibility of incidence among other groups hindered the development of an understanding of HIV transmission. It is now well understood to be related to specific behaviours, but epidemiological statistics continue to be recorded not in terms of the behaviours of needle-sharing and anal and vaginal intercourse, but in terms of groups labelled 'homosexual/bisexual' and 'intravenous drug user'. Those who are tested as having HIV antibodies and who can be classified under these labels are placed there on the assumption that they have contracted the virus through homosexual anal intercourse or needle-sharing if they have ever engaged in these practices, no matter how much heterosexual intercourse they may have had. The category of heterosexual transmission is accepted only if all other possibilities are exhausted, and most cases initially reported as 'heterosexual contact' are provisionally listed as 'other/undetermined'. This, of course, is only part of the much wider and deeper tendency in the discourse of HIV/AIDS to constitute it as deviant.

Strategies alternative to those based on physical control were already available when HIV/AIDS arrived, particularly in the field of women's health: health promotion based on preventive measures operates not through central uniform legal practices, but through dispersed educational programs focused on specific cultures and the meanings they give to health and disease (see Ballard 1988). The political context within which a choice of strategies for HIV/AIDS was exercised is significant. The Hawke Labor government came to

5 Sexuality and the State in Time of Epidemic

office early in 1983 just as the first case of AIDS in Australia was announced, and Labor's tradition of opposition to the medical profession as well as heated disputes over the establishment of Medicare and over doctors' salaries led the then Minister for Health, Neal Blewett, to develop a strategy of building alternative bases of policy advice in the Public Health Association, the women's health movement, the Consumer Health Forum and the Australian Federation of AIDS Organisations (Ballard 1989). Hence there was a predisposition towards culturally specific education through the AIDS Councils, a predisposition which did not obtain in the United States or the United Kingdom, with very different results in both policy and in continued transmission of HIV.

As in the case of many other state activities, if gay organizations had not existed prior to the HIV epidemic, it would have been necessary to call them into existence as the counterpart of government programs. Yet the AIDS Councils, established primarily by those who had been active on gay and lesbian issues in the 1970s, would not have been available to design and implement effective education programs without the prior mobilization of gay communities. Where other groups, identified initially in terms of 'risk', have not been previously mobilized, Australian governments—with the exception of those in Queensland and Tasmania until recently—have been willing to promote and finance the development of community-based programs. The national HIV/AIDS conference in Hobart in 1988 was used as the occasion for initiating group formation among people living with HIV/AIDS, among sex workers, organized nationally as the Scarlet Alliance, and among injecting drug users, organized as the Australian IV League. Co-optation is a risk for both sides in the negotiation of state support for communities, one which Foucault recognized in his discussions of power and sexuality (Graff 1989).

Perhaps the most interesting evidence of the varying impact of state action lies in the contrast between the national education programs on HIV/AIDS in television, radio and bus advertisements, and the community-based programs organized through the AIDS Councils and other groups. Both are government-financed but their attempts to shape sexuality are very different. From the Grim Reaper on, the national campaign assumed a common cultural understanding of sexuality among all Australians. Precisely because it is focused on the risks of penetrative sex it reinforces much of the standard authorized discourse of the patriarchal state. Community-based programs, which have received less funding than the national education program, have been predicated on the need for cultural specificity in education. Government investment in these programs was based on recognition that the state had no effective purchase on private sexual behaviour, but also on the political unacceptability of state programs addressing in sympathetic terms, and thus seen as accepting, 'deviant' sexualities. Given the evidence of substantial change in the sexual practices of urban gay communities, the education programs have proliferated and become increasingly differentiated as the finer distinctions in cultural diversity among ethnic groups, youth, the elderly and rural communities become recognized and, in a sense, incorporated.

The AIDS Councils' educational programs have also diversified to recognize the specificity of the sexualities of gay men in rural areas, working-class men in Sydney's western suburbs, and bisexual married men. This extension beyond the organized gay community has not taken place without some dislocation; though the search for safe sex has probably broadened the repertories of sexual expression, it has often proved difficult for committed gay men to cope with variations in sexuality beyond their own. Not unexpectedly the one cultural group, the unmarked category, whose sexuality remains relatively untouched by specific programs is that of heterosexual males, including most doctors, whose behaviour sets the cultural norm. Apart from the use of condoms they have not been encouraged to think about or to alter their sexual behaviour. Even the Commonwealth Government's comprehensive AIDS Policy Discussion Paper (Commonwealth of Australia 1988), in its listing of prevention strategies for 'priority groups', included those for adolescents and women, but omitted heterosexual men.

5 Sexuality and the State in Time of Epidemic

The Policy Discussion Paper was prelude to the *National HIV/AIDS Strategy*, issued as a Policy Information Paper (or White Paper) by the Commonwealth Government and tabled in all state parliaments (Commonwealth of Australia 1989). The impetus for the White Paper was primarily that of winning commitment to long-term funding for an agreed program by the Commonwealth and the states. But the earlier Policy Discussion Paper, which provided the basis for wide public discussion, had opened up the whole gamut of policy issues and ensured that the later White Paper provided an opportunity for global consideration of laws, policies and practice in all sectors of government with an impact on HIV/AIDS. The process of consultation and drafting forced a unified and public inspection of the implications of state action for sexuality in contexts ranging from prisons to immigration policy and thus linked together separate discourses and practices. The White Paper could not pull all of these into harmony—and it failed signally in the cases of immigration and the defence forces—but it established the basis for a later review of legislation relating to prostitution, homosexuality and discrimination on grounds of sexuality. This is proceeding under the aegis of the Intergovernmental Committee on AIDS, working closely with the Legal Working Group of the Australian Federation of AIDS Organisations to produce a comprehensive review of Commonwealth and state laws impinging on sexuality.

One feature of Australian political culture in the 1980s which has differentiated it from those of the United Kingdom and United States has been the relative weakness of the radical Christian right. Fred Nile and the tiny Call to Australia Party in New South Wales is a pale reflection of the family-based attack on gay rights led by Mary Whitehouse and Anita Bryant from the late 1970s. Labor governments in the Commonwealth and most states have had none of the disposition of the Thatcher and Reagan/Bush regimes to support a moral backlash against the communities most affected by HIV/AIDS. As a result there has been no equivalent of the Helms Amendment in the United States, barring the use of Federal funds for education on homosexuality, nor of the similar Clause 28 of the United Kingdom *Local Government Act 1988*; Weeks argues in the case of Clause 28 that 'far from diminishing the public presence of lesbians and gay men it greatly contributed to an enhanced sense of identity and community' (1991: 216). In the absence of a strong political force in Australia mobilized against divergent sexuality, it has been the leading spokesmen of the medical profession, dispossessed of their rightful pre-eminence in advice on all health issues, who have challenged the purported influence of 'the gay lobby' on the Commonwealth Government's HIV/AIDS policies (Ballard 1989).

The net effect of the national and community programs on HIV/AIDS has been to produce an extraordinary expansion in public awareness through an explosion of explicit discourse on sexuality, reinforcing the central discourse on penetrative heterosexuality, yet recognizing and legitimating diversity in sexual behaviour. This legitimation, together with the program of legal change being pushed through with an HIV/AIDS rationale, may be displacing the Wolfenden dispensation. It would be premature to argue that the moral taxonomy of compulsory public heterosexuality and private choice in sexuality has been abandoned, but the gay and lesbian program of the 1970s has been sufficiently taken up as a public and state-authorized discourse so that it would be difficult to reinstate an earlier regime.

6

THE 'PRESENT MOMENT' IN SEXUAL POLITICS

Jill Julius Matthews

The historian Edward Shorter has argued that most European women who lived before 1850 were never afflicted with venereal diseases, and those who were tended to belong to marginal and endogamous groups. After that date, however, the diseases crossed the boundaries into the respectable classes. Put simply, from late in the eighteenth century until the middle of the twentieth century there was a long, slow increase in frequency and dispersal of infection, with things getting considerably worse for women of all classes in the last quarter of the nineteenth century. While acknowledging the shakiness of the statistics, Shorter opts for a prevalence of venereal diseases in Britain at the turn of the century of around four women infected per thousand. Rates of infection increased in first half of the twentieth century, with effective treatment of gonorrhoea not available until well after the discovery of sulpha drugs in 1936; syphilis had to wait for penicillin, after 1943 (Shorter 1982: 263–7). Reporting in 1916, the British Royal Commission on Venereal Diseases had estimated that 'the number of persons who have been infected with syphilis, acquired or congenital, cannot fall below ten per cent of the whole population in the large cities, and the percentage infected with gonorrhoea must greatly exceed this proportion' (cited in Rosen 1974: 205–6). Walkowitz, writing in 1980, claims that, according to her reading of available statistics, syphilis must have been endemic to the civilian population in Great Britain in the Victorian and Edwardian eras (Walkowitz 1980: 50).

The Australian story of venereal disease corresponds with Shorter's chronology. Syphilis and gonorrhoea arrived in Australia in 1788 with the convicts and troops of the First Fleet (Siedlecky and Wyndham 1990: 115). The Aboriginal population was immediately infected, and the rapid decline in the Aboriginal birth rate following invasion has been attributed to the ravages of the disease (Butlin 1983: 37–41, 77–9). By 1904 the Royal Commission on the Decline in the Birth-Rate and on the Mortality of Infants in New South Wales, only interested in the white population and much more concerned with children than their mothers, declared that venereal disease was 'the third main reason, after abortion and the use of contraceptives, for New South Wales' declining birth-rate', and was the cause of 'at least 60 per 1000 babies treated at the Sydney Hospital for Sick Children' dying in their first month (Siedlecky and Wyndham 1990: 114).

During World War I, New Zealand feminist sex reformer Ettie Rout was condemned by one of the bishops in the House of Lords as 'the most wicked woman in Britain' for distributing condoms to colonial troops in Egypt and on leave in Paris (Hornibrook n.d. [1935]: 113). Rout's work was based in a belief in sex idealism, wherein woman's body was a temple enlivened by a eugenic instinct which needed to be protected by science; the enemy was composed of individuals and groups with an 'obscenity complex' who sought to enforce an ignorance of sex hygiene (Rout n.d. [1925]: 17–20). Meanwhile, other Australasian feminist sex reformers, such as Angela Booth, campaigned vigorously against any distribution of condoms to the troops, arguing that prophylactics would merely encourage promiscuity and that only a change in male attitudes would curb the disease (Radi n.d. [1988]: 87).

A British feminist, writing on the eve of World War I, had developed a broader analysis of the sexual politics of venereal disease. Christabel Pankhurst, in her major work *The Great Scourge and How to End It*, described the desperate

6 The 'Present Moment' in Sexual Politics

dialectic of disease and oppression: 'The cause of sexual disease is the subjection of women'. She argued that most of the physical weaknesses and ailments of women were due to gonorrhoeal infection, not to natural weakness. Thus, Victorian women's apparent frailty was initially a consequence and not a cause, as was so often argued, of their being kept subordinate to men. It then became a cause of further indignities, of enforced ignorance, and of the denial of freedom to take care of themselves. 'This canker of venereal disease is eating away the vitals of the nation, and the only cure is Votes for Women, which is to say the recognition of the freedom and human equality of women' (Pankhurst 1913). Men must change, ignorance must be swept away, and women must be set free: 'Votes for Women, Chastity for Men'.

Meanwhile, in these years around World War I, a dance craze was sweeping the Western world and its colonies. Ragtime, tango and jazz emerged from the nights of Harlem and Rio into the white of day. In cabarets and cafes and pie shops, in Palais de Danse and Salons de Luxe and Tango Tea Rooms, young people engaged en masse in lascivious, promiscuous, sexually explicit bodily movement: the Bunny Hug, the Grizzly Bear, the Turkey Trot, the Black Bottom. From 1910 to World War II and after, dance floors were sites of fierce debate and even violent confrontation between the shifting alliances of capitalists and hedonists, artists and guardians of civic decency, policemen and churchmen, policewomen and feminists, and a lot of young people who were out to have a good time. In Ireland, an archbishop threatened to excommunicate people who frequented all-night dances, while in Australia the Methodist Church banned mixed dancing in church halls (*West Australian* 26 August 1925; Bisset 1979: 38).

All sides to the public debates tended to operate within a moral world ordered by similar, self-evident truths, the most central of which concerned pleasure. Pursuit of pleasure for its own sake was held in contempt by all. It was recognized as almost an instinct, a drive: 'They must dance

... it is almost as natural as the desire for food and sleep' (Marbury 1914: 25). But, as a drive, it operated according to a law of entropy, drawing inevitably towards 'suggestive ideas and unworthy ideals' (Marbury 1914: 25), pulling down the pillars of civilization. It must, therefore, be tamed and harnessed to worthy ends and uplifting values, or it must be banned in the name of those values. All this was agreed; it was only the particular qualities of the desired ends and values that divided the combatants in the diatribes of the dance.

Among the leaders of the international pro-dance lobby were Irene and Vernon Castle, whose self-appointed mission was to de-sexualize and make respectable modern dancing. The proclaimed aim of their book, *Modern Dancing* (1914), was 'to uplift dancing, purify it, and place it before the public in its proper light' (Castle 1914: 17). In the book's introduction, New York socialite–intellectual, Bessie Marbury, held out the value of dancing over other less worthy pleasures:

> Surely there cannot be as great moral danger in dancing as there is in sitting huddled close in the darkness of a sensational moving-picture show or in following with feverish interest the suggestive sex-problem dramas. Nor from my point of view is there as much harm in dancing as in sitting home in some dreary little hall bedroom, beneath the flaring gas, reading with avidity the latest erotic novel or the story which paints vice in alluring colors under the guise of describing life as it really is. (Marbury 1914: 22–3)

There were, of course, styles of dancing that Bessie Marbury did not countenance, most particularly vulgar musical comedy and vaudeville dancing. And there were many pleasures of the dance she did not mention at all, including the mannish women dancing with their girlfriends in the clubs and bars of Paris, Greenwich Village, and Sydney.

While shady women and bright young things and business girls and factory girls jazzed to a syncopated rhythm, and while their elders discoursed upon pleasure and disease and education, in her chair in Monk's House, Virginia Woolf played with Orlando and prefigured Foucault's 'repressive hypothesis'.

6 The 'Present Moment' in Sexual Politics

> The great cloud which hung, not only over London, but over the whole of the British Isles on the first day of the nineteenth century stayed ... [S]teadily and imperceptibly, none marking the exact day or hour of the change, the constitution of England was altered and nobody knew it ... The damp struck within. Men felt the chill in their hearts; the damp in their minds. In a desperate effort to snuggle their feelings into some sort of warmth one subterfuge was tried after another. Love, birth, and death were all swaddled in a variety of fine phrases. The sexes drew further and further apart. No open conversation was tolerated. Evasions and concealments were sedulously practised on both sides. And just as the ivy and the evergreen rioted in the damp earth outside, so did the same fertility show itself within. The life of the average woman was a succession of childbirths. (Woolf 1977 [1928]: 142–3)

Woolf characterizes the spirit of the Victorian age as damp, fecund, hideous, sentimental, prudish, censorious, and indissolubly coupled. Then, upon the death of the Queen, the clouds of the age lift and a brittle brightness succeeds with Edward. So Woolf comes to the present moment, and her hero/ine turns pale: 'For what more terrifying revelation can there be than that it is the present moment? That we survive the shock at all is only possible because the past shelters us on one side and the future on another' (Woolf 1977 [1928]: 186–7).

More than sixty years later, here, now, what on earth do all these ancient matters have to do with this present terrifying moment, the present moment in sexual politics? Why raise at all these matters of venereal disease and 1920s jazz and Victorianism? There are always many reasons to invoke the past. Here, I wish briefly to discuss four.

A NEW PRESENT CREATES A NEW PAST

Intense consciousness of HIV/AIDS throughout the 1980s, in conjunction with the re-orientation of historiography through feminist scholarship, has meant that there is now the possibility of a generation come to consciousness on this side of the 1960s sexual revolution being able to understand in new ways the meanings of sexuality, feminism and sexual politics in the pre-penicillin era, the meanings of women's lives in a time of plague without cure. From this point of vantage, historians may now hear in a different way the words of past women and men explaining themselves; may now speak of the sexual politics of the past, using words not already soggy from too-long immersion in Victorian truth. The historicity of the meanings of sexuality are made clear in ways not available before.

An instance of this is in the way in which understandings of the nineteenth-century British and American women's movements are currently undergoing substantial revision. (See, for example, the major work by Kent *Sex and Suffrage in Britain 1860–1914* (1987), and the discussion by DuBois (1991) of 'Eleanor Flexner and the History of American Feminism'.) Historians are beginning to employ notions of sexual politics that were unavailable while the concept of rigidly separated public and private spheres held sway, a concept effectively elaborated as a truth by the Victorians, and still employed as such today. They are also able to employ notions that were unavailable while the concepts of sexuality as liberation, as the truth of one's identity held sway, concepts that had a strong secret life from the late nineteenth century and emerged to enjoy their heyday from the late 1950s into the 1980s. That part of the women's movement that had seemed, to such libertarian consciousness, to be marginal, a moral purity crusade motivated by a censorious prudishness, can now be reinterpreted as the central aim of a fully integrated political campaign to transform the gender order and redefine all relationships between women and men, both public and private (Kent 1987: 3–16). Not yet fully developed in such revisions, but certainly informing the sensibilities of their authors, is a new understanding of possible meanings in a social and psychic world gripped by endemic, incurable, sexually transmitted disease. (Early work specifically based in comparisons between syphilis and HIV infection includes Susan Sontag's (1989) *AIDS and Its Metaphors* and Elaine Showalter's (1990) *Sexual Anarchy*.)

6 The 'Present Moment' in Sexual Politics

OLD PASTS ARE STILL PRESENT

While such new ways of speaking of sexual politics in the past are beginning, the old ways still continue strongly into the present moment. Woolf's damp and fecund Victorian discourses have had a long life, and linger today despite considerable permutation. What was then called wowserism[1] and is now called moralism, whether expressed by doctors, clerics, politicians, feminists, or the populist right; what was then and is still called libertarianism, whether expressed by sexual radicals, pornographers, feminists, or the populist left: these discourses have survived at least a century and a half. Moreover, despite their trenchant mutual opposition over all that time, they are deeply intertwined, sharing many continuities of concern and concept. Most particularly, both the moral and the libertarian discourses are ruled by similar rigid dichotomies which constitute much of the common sense of current debates around sexual politics: purity and pleasure, order and individuality, temperance and promiscuity, Agape and Eros, repression and disease, duties and rights, civilization and freedom. Only the particular positioning of each protagonist as fulcrum balancing the normative extremes differs.

Thus, the general enterprise that Bersani has termed the 'redemptive reinvention of sex' with its 'pastoralizing project' (Bersani 1988: 215, 221), and that I have discussed in terms of the contempt for pleasure for its own sake, still rules the discourse of sexuality. That discourse is incapable of anything but condemnation of sexual behaviour that cannot be recuperated for worthy social ends, whether they be heterosexual reproduction or ideologically sound liberation politics. It is incapable of 'the willing suspension of disbelief ... that constitutes poetic faith' (Coleridge 1817), that admits of unredeemed pleasure. Such an official, public discourse is itself a sexual politics, one which denies other understandings of sexuality; for example, that alluded to by gay activist, Ken Davis:

> Lesbians and gays are not always well behaved in public, sober, sane and comfortably housed. Sometimes we do want to fuck

in parks and toilets, use illegal drugs, stage confrontational demos, sell sex for money, cavort with 'underage' friends, offend decent people and frighten the horses. (Davis 1990)

Yet, even here, there is more a sense of thumbing one's nose at respectable society, a libertarian gesture, than of pleasure for its own sake. The discursive public space of sexuality is thoroughly colonized by the functional meanings of pleasure in the moralist–libertarian debate. There is no language in which to justify behaviour as simply pleasurable, without reducing it to false consciousness or to ecstasy. There are barely words in which even to speak of it, only absences: reckless, irresponsible, careless. Such behaviour is marginal to discourse, it is inarticulate, it is incomprehensible; it is necessarily outside the law in all its senses. It is the moment before being caught, of which all one can say is, 'I didn't think', 'I forgot', 'I got carried away'. I am not, of course, suggesting by this discussion that pleasure for its own sake is nice, that it is a good thing, or to be encouraged. Rather, I am alluding to a dimension of sexuality which is a necessary part of sexual politics but which is beyond calculation.

WHAT'S IN A NAME?

A third point deriving from the ancient matters is that sexuality is not one thing. It is not even one thing for men and another for women, or one thing for gays and another for straights, or one thing for scientists and another for laypeople. Sexuality is always more than one can or would wish to imagine, because it exists in the confluence of unconscious desire and the vagaries of social relations. A norm of sexuality was established by the taxonomic sexologists of the late nineteenth century, a curious understanding of activity and passivity, of penis in vagina. Everything else became a perversion, a deviation from the norm, but was nonetheless sexuality. As Bessie Marbury well understood, sexuality is dirty dancing; it is also reading an erotic novel, watching drama or cinema. These are not sublimations of sexuality, they are its forms.

The penis-in-vagina form, of course, still constitutes the truth of sexuality in the public common sense of the West although, especially since the 1920s' popularization of Freud and sexology, this structural understanding of sexuality has been supplemented by a functional component, namely orgasm. Sexuality is what gives you an orgasm. But then comes the problem that while there is a structural–functional fit for most men, the normal form is found not necessarily, or even very often, to provide an orgasm for women. Moreover, while representations of penis-in-vagina are reputed to be sexually arousing for many men, for many women pictures of food are described as producing similar tumescence of bodily organs, as 'mouth-watering'. Meanwhile, there is an enormous internal debate among lesbian feminists as to what exactly is lesbian sexuality, if definitions based on genital contact are deemed a masculine obsession. In other words, the central terms of the debates about sexuality and sexual politics have been fastened to a particular understanding of masculine heterosexuality, and need to be unloosened. The question is not only what is sexuality. In addition, we need to know who is asking the question and who is giving the answer and for what purposes. What are the positions of the disputants? What have been the bodily experiences and fantasies that set their boundaries of meaning? In what networks of power have they played, in what network are they currently playing?

WHAT'S AT STAKE?

Finally, and cumulatively, the ancient matters establish what is at stake in the Anglophone debates about sexuality and sexual politics that have existed since women first began to speak publicly and collectively of sexual matters, in the 1860s. The stakes are Pleasure, Fear, and Obligation. It is the linking of these terms that makes pleasure for its own sake an almost incomprehensible concept; that makes sexuality such a broad category; and that makes any social, let alone personal, understanding of sexual politics such a complex and tenuous enterprise.

It is easy enough to list under each of those headings the issues that would need investigation in the present moment of sexual politics. Under pleasure would come specific bodily, emotional, mental and aesthetic sensations, the range of available methods to obtain them, and the nature of the relationships they organize. The demographic and social profile of contemporary women creates a filigree grid upon which one would seek to understand passion and lust, companionability, desiring, being desired, having fun and contentedly or desperately seeking. Countering pleasure is the list of fears: sometimes pregnancy; always disease. There are still the old tried and true syphilis and gonorrhoea, but the list is ever-expanding: herpes, genital warts, pelvic inflammatory disease, cervical cancer, HIV infection. Sexual interaction can entail pain and being hurt. Interactions with the wrong people can lead to punishment by regulatory agencies: police, welfare, education, medicine, law. Always there is the fear of loss of love, withdrawal of affection, desire displaced.

Sexual politics have often been understood as a tension between these two apparent opposites, pleasure and fear. Indeed, in much recent feminist argument they have been turned into sites to defend and from which to attack, with social constructionist feminists or sexual libertarians defending pleasure against the radical feminists or sexual pessimists for whom sex is fear (for example, Valverde (1987); Vance (1984); cf. Leidholdt and Raymond (1990)). Yet it would seem more useful to step away from this by now rather static tension and add a third term, obligation, as a means of recasting an understanding of sexual politics.

Obligation introduces a dimension of power, of movement and interrelation into the discussion. In terms of sexuality, as of all else, women are embedded in a network of power relations, and their position in that network is usually incoherent. That is to say, women occupy a series of positions in a multitude of discourses and practices, and those positions are not necessarily compatible and are often contradictory. Most of these contemporary discourses share a similar vocabulary of liberal humanism, with its concepts of rights and duties, of obligation. It is the variety of people

6 The 'Present Moment' in Sexual Politics

or relationships to whom obligation is owed, and the emotional quality of what is owed that creates the contradictions and incoherence. The power of obligation flows back and forth between the positions created by the relationships: mother to child, wife to husband, partner to partner, daughter to parent, friend to friend, worker to colleague, worker to employer, expert to client, supplicant or deviant to a variety of state agencies and professional authorities. There is as well the obligation to self, an obligation still difficult to conceptualize as women continue to seek entry to the liberal individualist paradigm from which they were originally deliberately excluded (Pateman 1988). The obligation to self ranges from a concern for self-survival or security through to a more intangible notion of self-determination or autonomy.

In this contractual world of emotional and physical rights and obligations, sexuality is a manifold capacity. It can be commodified and exchanged or sold—for food, shelter, money—in such ways as to leave intact the self. Alternatively, it can be constituted as part of the self itself, and given wholly to another's keeping as a gift with or without the expectation of reciprocity. Again, it can be provided as fealty to the superior other or demanded from the inferior. Women engage their sexuality in these many ways, and there is no single position that constitutes the real state of sexual politics today.

Or perhaps there is. What many writers have identified as the ideology of compulsory heterosexuality runs consistently through these multiple positions and practices (Rich 1980). The reproductive obligation which used to be indissolubly linked to that heterosexuality has loosened somewhat and, while still centrally important, is no longer imperative for women. And, indeed, there is even some shift in the heterosexuality demanded, with the possibility of discreet and occasional homosexuality for individuals. What has not shifted is the obligation women as individuals and as a group owe men in their institutional incarnations (that is, as men rather than masculine persons), whether individually or as a group. In other words, at particular times there may be relations between individuals that are relatively free of obligation, where gender is a more or less personal attribute. More often, it is heterosexuality as an institution that calls individuals to occupy given positions in a given relationship, such as those listed above. In such relationships, even of lover to lover, the lines of power and of obligation are already set up according to the hierarchical ordering of male-dominant heterosexuality. One cannot be simply an individual, but must become a woman of a particular sort, fit to occupy the particular position. There is, of course, considerable individual freedom as to how one may perform the obligations of the relationship, but the boundaries of the possible are firm and pre-determined.

An example of this can be shown through studies of young women's sexuality. What little research interest there has been in this area has often been guided by a concern with possible policy interventions, in particular to prevent juvenile pregnancy (Lees 1986: 14–28). Such concern has recently become more urgent in the face of the need to ensure safe sexual practices to protect against HIV infection. Much has been written by researchers about the obsession of young adolescent women to get and keep a boyfriend, and the tumultuous and dangerous contradictions between pleasure and fear into which they often fall. Certainly, the pleasures and dangers are real enough, but to see the situation solely in these terms tends to create an understanding based on notions of wilful individualism, of ignorance, irresponsibility and peer pressure. Adding the notion of the obligation of compulsory heterosexuality allows us to broaden the range of possible interpretation.

For a teenage girl, in most instances, the need for the boyfriend is only secondarily about desire for any particular boy; primarily, it is about creating an adult posture for herself by fitting into the pre-existing, approved, institutionalized mode of being a young woman. Central to that mode is compulsory heterosexuality, which is in general a hierarchical mode of male dominance, although, again, there can be considerable flexibility within its boundaries. In certain crucial areas, however, particularly to do with genital sexual experimentation, the young woman is con-

6 The 'Present Moment' in Sexual Politics

stituted by the relationship itself as subordinate, with little power to initiate or demur. But this particular inferiority is of limited importance weighed against the meaning of the relationship itself. For the young woman, conforming herself to the model is the easiest and often only apparent way from here to there. Her path to successful heterosexual adulthood lies through her willing acceptance of the obligation to do whatever is necessary to sustain the mode. No particular boyfriend is indispensible, but a boyfriend she must have and, since all the available ones at school or in the neighbourhood tend to share a similar culture of masculinity, as a consequence she may well engage in unsafe sexual practices demanded by any particular boyfriend. What may stand against her conforming will be not an intrinsic moral rectitude but the power of obligation she owes in other social relationships. But, importantly, such relationships will have to speak directly to the maintenance of compulsory heterosexuality and the achievement of womanhood.

'Good' as distinct from 'delinquent' adolescent girls who engage in dangerous sexual practices have generally been judged to be ignorant and lacking in confidence: conditions to be overcome by information and education in assertiveness. Education here is understood to be the instruction of an individual, a rational agent, a self-determining subject: effectively, a man. But a young woman knows that she won't get a boyfriend if she's a man. She is embraced in a relationship with her future that obliges her at this moment not to be assertive, not to initiate, not to say 'no', or 'if it's not on, it's not on'. The problem, in other words, lies not in her lack of confidence but in the obligations of institutional, hierarchical heterosexuality which presents itself as the truth of femininity as well as the truth of sex. There are no other available obliging relations that call her into normal adulthood.

The solution? If this is indeed the correct problem, then the answer lies in the words of the much-maligned Christabel Pankhurst: 'Votes for Women, which is to say the recognition of the freedom and human equality of women'.

NOTE

[1] 'Wowser' is a quintessentially Australian word, probably invented by John Norton, editor of the Sydney *Truth*, around 1900. Its clearest definition, however, comes from the American lexicographer, H. L. Mencken: 'A drab souled Philistine haunted by the mockery of others' happiness. Every Puritan is not necessarily a wowser; to be one he must devote himself zealously to reforming the morals of his neighbours, and, in particular, to throwing obstacles in the way of their enjoyment of what they choose to regard as pleasures' (Dunstan 1968: 2).

7

HUMAN SEXUALITY IN AUSTRALIA: THE QUEST FOR INFORMATION

John S. Western

INTRODUCTION

As John Gagnon noted some fifteen years ago, a deliberate concern for the role of sexuality in human life has a relatively short history, one of scarcely a century, at least in so far as that concern takes as its point of departure an attempt at disclosing what people do sexually through systematic research which is consistent with the basic canons of scientific inquiry (Gagnon 1975: 113).

Gagnon goes on to suggest that toward the end of the nineteenth century in Europe a major cultural movement emerged that directly challenged previously held beliefs about the role of the sexual in human life. It was at that time that the works of Freud, Hirschfeld, Moll and Krafft-Ebing on the continent and Havelock Ellis in England began to appear in print. This movement shared elements and overlapped with changing patterns of political and artistic thought and activity. It was part of the period in cultural history which was the source of the ideas and experience of the 'modern'. Gagnon continues that if there was a basic common ground in the work of this generation, it was that they acted to move sexuality out of the domain of the alien and the ignored, and to bring sexual acts and actors into the world of the noticed.

The scientific works that began to appear at this time were a challenge to many of the collective views on the place of sex in human life. The extended crisis created by the Freudian position and its vast intellectual influence resulted from the decision of its adherents to place sexuality at the centre of character formation, not as an undesirable instinct that could and should be controlled, but as a prime motive force, bringing about the development of cultural life itself. In contrast to Freud, Havelock Ellis argued for a more selective impact of the role of the sexual. He focused on dispelling ignorance and superstition about sexual matters, and emphasized education and reform.

Gagnon provides a comprehensive analysis of the early influences of these two and other researchers of the time. He notes that the sexual situation in the United States during these years was perhaps more conservative than in Europe and that, by the turn of the century, the United States remained largely dependent on European ideas. Indeed, the work of Freud, Ellis and others came to be modestly well known between 1900 and 1920, to an urban and academic élite only.

It was during the 1920s that research into sexual conduct began in the United States in a systematic way, Gagnon notes. Partially under the influence of Freud and variants of psychoanalytic doctrine, but more importantly as a reflection of various social reform movements in the United States, three studies of the sexual behaviour of those with relatively conventional sexual lives were completed. In 1929, Catherine Davis published a questionnaire study entitled *Factors in the Sex Life of 2,200 Women*, a study begun in 1920 and initiating a tradition of the recording of the sexual lives of the college-educated. George Hamilton conducted interviews with 200 men and women, the results of which were also published in 1929 entitled *A Study in Marriage*, and Robert Dickinson and Louise Beam published in 1932 research drawn from Dickinson's files as a gynaecologist, entitled *One Thousand Marriages*.

All three works, while showing evidence of a continuing European influence, reflected as well the social conditions of the United States. These studies anticipated what was to become, at least for a time, an American hegemony in empirical research on sexual behaviour. The use of structured questionnaires, the anticipation of scientific sampling and the presentation of data in tabular and statistical format made this work the direct ancestor of Kinsey's research as well as of other sexual studies of a survey nature.

Much of the research prior to this time had been in the case-history or clinical form—a form that Gagnon claimed took as its model works of literature and the imagination. The findings of these and related studies exposed a partial picture of sexual conduct, at least in the middle class. What appeared was a picture of conventional individuals trying to work out their own sexual lives in a situation of profound personal ignorance, misinformation and cultural isolation. This was the social climate in which Freudian psychoanalysis found a home, not necessarily as an acceptable doctrine, but as a *cause célèbre* around which multi-faceted argument could take place.

THE KINSEY STUDIES

It was at this time when psychoanalysis and related conceptualizations were becoming more widespread in the United States that Kinsey began his own research on human sexuality. Versions of the Kinsey story are relatively well known. Kinsey, already a well-established researcher in evolutionary theory based on studies of the ecology and gross morphological structure of gall wasps, was asked to give sex instruction as part of a marriage guidance course. Dissatisfied with the state of knowledge about this aspect of that course, he began to study sexual behaviour. There are two areas of Kinsey's work to comment briefly on: methodology and the incidence, range and social patterning of sexuality.

Methodology

The Kinsey studies were based on a number of surveys involving in all about 20 000 respondents. The studies were the earliest of the few large sample surveys of sexuality. Highly controversial at the time, Kinsey's methods have raised questions under two broad sub-headings: sampling and measurement. The major criticisms of the Kinsey sample concerned the fact that the respondents were volunteers rather than randomly selected (Brecher 1969: 140).

Volunteer bias has been a recurrent theme in both the psychological and psycho-sociological branches of sex research (see, for example, Wolchik et al. 1983; and the comments of Reiss 1983), and the recognized bias introduced by self-selection has led some researchers to use random sampling techniques (Reiss 1967; Zelnik and Katner 1977, 1980; Wyatt et al. 1988).

While considering the problems of sampling in some depth, Kinsey gave only limited attention to the problem of measurement. Kinsey's measure of sexual preference, a seven-point scale ranging from 'entirely heterosexual' to 'entirely homosexual' (Kinsey et al. 1953), is a manifest item intended to tap a latent variable. Since Kinsey, a range of linear scales and more sophisticated multi-dimensional measures have been developed.

The measurement of sexual preference has been recast by a number of writers in the area of bisexuality. Rejecting the Kinsey assumption that bisexuality was a sexual identity 'mid-way' between homosexuality and heterosexuality, Hansen and Evans (1985) proposed a two-dimensional definition of sexuality involving sex-aim and emotional quality. A more elaborate model of sexual identity was suggested by Klein et al. (1985) whose measure is based on seven variables with a dynamic component.

A number of other multi-dimensional scales have been proposed and utilized in several other areas. For example, Hendrick and Hendrick (1987), drawing on psychometrics, developed a measure of sexual attitudes based on the dimensions of permissiveness, pre-marital sex and the 'meaning' of sexuality. Sexual activity has been measured in terms of relationship, commitment, orgasm consistency, frequency of intercourse and effectiveness of contraceptive devices (Pinney et al. 1987). Reviews of different scales of sexual practices and attitudes can be found in Schiavi et al. (1979).

Social patterning of sexual activity and attitudes

Kinsey's analysis of sexuality can be divided into three main areas: sexual socialization, various modes of sexual expression and the relationship between social structure and sexuality. Each of these areas has developed extensively since Kinsey's early studies.

A large part of the literature examining sexuality as an outcome of social learning has concentrated on the incidence and effects of sexual experience among children and the sexual practices and attitudes of adolescents. The discussion of sexual socialization among children typically examined the harmful consequences of childhood sexual experience (Fritz et al. 1981; Sgroi 1978; Gagnon 1965). The sexual awareness of children has also been studied (Langfeldt 1980).

American research into the sexual socialization of adolescents has been wide-ranging. Inquiries into adolescent sexuality have frequently analyzed attitudes to, and the prevalence of, premarital intercourse (DeLamater and MacCorqodale 1979; Robinson and Jedlicka 1982; Singh 1980). Another important topic of study concerns adolescents' knowledge and use of contraceptives (Milan and Kilman 1987).

Kinsey suggested that the range of 'sexual outlets' was strongly related to the socialization process. While heterosexual activity has always received the majority of academic attention, bisexuality and homosexuality have also received extended treatment and were found to be relatively common in the United States (Klein and Wolf 1985; MacInnes 1973). Similar findings exist in the research on taboo sexual practices such as paedophilia, and practices commonly regarded as unconventional such as sado-masochism (Araji and Finkelhor 1986; Gosselin and Wilson 1980).

Given modes of sexual expression are formed in particular circumstances. Henslin argues: 'it is [individuals'] group membership that shapes, directs and influences the forms or patterns their sexual behaviours take' (1971, 1–2). This premise has informed a wide variety of research, which has included investigations into the relationship between race and sexuality (Day 1972), permissiveness and class (Reiss 1967) and sex and occupation (Cummins 1971). Most current research today routinely includes demographic variables in the analysis precisely because of the recognized importance of social patterns of sexuality.

THE STUDY OF HUMAN SEXUALITY IN AUSTRALIA

The significant methodological and substantive issues raised in the more recent American literature have been only partially addressed in Australia. Frequently the Australian research has lacked familiarity with the more sophisticated issues surrounding instrument design and survey administration. Australian researchers have also tended to explore a much narrower range of questions than their American counterparts.

Methodology

In Australia, fewer studies of sexuality have been based on random samples, although the problems of sample bias have been recognized (Ross 1982). Research in Australia using random sampling has focused on highly specific research questions involving respondents with distinctive demographic characteristics (e.g. Wilson 1979; McCabe 1987; Trlin et al. 1983). A significant exception to this has been the National AIDS Education Campaign's *Benchmark Survey* (Commonwealth Department of Community Services and Health 1988). While the national sample drawn in this survey was more thorough than in any previous research on sexual practices in Australia, the substantive focus of the survey, HIV/AIDS, was more limited than a broad-ranging, Kinsey-style study would have been.

Australian research has been largely unresponsive to the developments in multi-dimensional measurement indicating the need for extensive research in this area. A number of recent studies (e.g. Ross 1982) have retained the Kinsey scale of sexual identity or used single-item attitude scales (e.g. Brumby 1983). Despite this trend, a few studies have moved towards the use of multi-dimensional attitude measures. Hong (1983) has modelled attitudes to homosexuality along two axes: social–personal acceptance and perceived normality. He urges that further studies should use multi-dimensional instruments. It is clear from this brief

7 Human Sexuality in Australia

review that work on Australian sexuality urgently requires an investigation of various research strategies.

Social patterning of sexual activity and attitudes

Australian research on sexual activity and attitudes has little of the variety and depth of the American studies. In Australia, most research has concentrated on children and adolescents. While this has been very limited in scope, it points to the substantial policy significance of this line of investigation.

In Australia, most of the literature on the sexual experience of children has focused on the prevalence and effects of child abuse. Goldman and Goldman (1988) found that significant numbers of their sample of Victorian tertiary students experienced sexual abuse as children. In a related study (Goldman and Goldman 1984), they argued that this experience impeded normal sexual development and suggested that more research is urgently needed in the area. Other studies published in Australia have looked at the effects of abuse and incest on childbirth (Areskig et al. 1983) and sexual dysfunction (Becker et al. 1982).

Studies of adolescent sexuality are overwhelmingly concerned with attitudes to, and experience with, premarital sex and contraception. A substantial proportion of Australian teenagers are sexually active, although no estimate is available. Sexual behaviour is largely determined by expectations of peer behaviour (Collins and Harper 1985) and attitudes to premarital virginity (Trlin et al. 1983). About half of Australian teenagers used no contraception at their first intercourse and continue to have sex without contraception (Kovacs et al. 1986; Collins and Robinson 1986).

Adolescent sexual attitudes vary across a range of factors. Gender differences account for sizeable variations in attitudes to contraception (Collins and Robinson 1986; see also Chapman and Hodgson 1988; Krishnamoorthy et al. 1983), desired family size (Callan and Wilks 1982) and concern with HIV/AIDS (Peterson and Peterson 1987). McCabe and Collins (1983) found that age, religiosity and type of school were all important predictors of sexual attitudes of Australian adolescents. The importance of religiosity has been doubted by Collins and Robinson (1986).

In the absence of a comprehensive database, surveys involving samples of the entire population have looked at attitudes to abortion (Fraser and Fraser 1982), sexual permissiveness (Hong 1985), homosexuality (Hong 1983) and HIV/AIDS (Commonwealth Department of Community Services and Health 1988). The limited range of empirical questions explored by Australian researchers is hampered by the absence of any national statistics concerning sexual practices. This underlines the importance of a study of the issues underlying the preparation of such a set of statistics.

UNITED STATES AND AUSTRALIA COMPARED: IMPLICATIONS FOR FURTHER RESEARCH

Unlike the United States, Australia has had no broad large-scale survey of sexual activity and attitudes. Data on scientific modes of sexual expression and their distribution and patterning are significant absences in the information available on sexuality in Australia. Each of these areas raises important health and policy questions.

What little research there is has been limited by small, targeted and often self-selected samples and relatively unsophisticated survey instruments. While suggestive of a number of directions for government strategy, this work has resulted in patchy and sometimes conflicting findings in a narrow range of areas.

Finally, several areas which are suggestive of new research agendas have attracted a great deal of attention. These areas include practices and attitudes surrounding sexually transmissible diseases (Zinner 1985; in Australia, Commonwealth Department of Community Services and Health 1988; Kippax, Crawford, Dowsett et al. 1990), fertility and reproductive technology (Singer and Wells 1985; Arditti et al. 1984) and sexual politics (Connell 1987; Weeks 1985).

These recent developments, the state of Australian research and the social policy significance of such research point to the urgent need for a broad national study. Such a study would need to be prefaced by a careful examination of competing methodologies and theoretical perspectives.

THE CASE FOR, AND NATURE OF, A LARGE-SCALE STUDY OF HUMAN SEXUALITY IN AUSTRALIA

Knowledge of the extent, diversity and patterns of change in sexual expression are rudimentary to non-existent at a community and national level in Australia. There are many health and related policy concerns raised by existing patterns of sexuality and sexual expression. These problems impose a major social and economic burden on the community in terms of family breakdown, unwanted and/or unplanned pregnancies, sexually transmitted diseases, psychiatric and sexual counselling services and the like. A broadly based study of human sexuality would provide the baseline data necessary for the development of balanced and informed policy options. In addition, similar projects are underway in other developed and developing countries, and Australian data would provide essential complimentary information for our unique population structure.

While simultaneously opening the way for broadly based comparative analyses, such a national study should not be simply a replication of the Kinsey study of the 1930s and 1940s. Kinsey's study was largely taxonomic and attempted to describe and classify a range of sexual behaviours. The aim of an Australian study should not be simply to describe the range of sexual behaviours, but to locate such behaviours in the underlying social conditions which gave rise to them.

In addition, contemporary sexological research has tended to concentrate on point prevalence rather than lifetime rates of sexual behaviours as an estimate of frequency of occurrence, and on the use of truncated recall periods (weeks or months) to provide adequate reliability rather than over lifetimes as Kinsey did. Further, the use of sexual diaries as trialled by Coxon (1988) has proved to be a useful, reliable and valid tool for measurement of sexual histories, when combined with an interview to clarify the methodology.

The recent Economic and Social Research Council seminar, 'Issues in Researching Sexual Behaviour', published in the *Joint Centre for Survey Methods Newsletter* (Volume 10, No. 1) also looked at recent methodological developments. A paper by Field and Wadsworth (1989/90) outlined the development of a methodology for a national survey of 'Sexual Attitudes' and a further paper by Davies (1989/90) discussed personal interviews with diary-keeping to provide improved measures of sexual behaviour. McQueen (1989/90) looked at the stability and consistency of sensitive information obtained from face-to-face and computer-assisted telephone interviews, while Orton and Quick (1989/90) reported on monitoring attitudes and behaviour in response to HIV/AIDS. Clearly a great deal of work using advanced methodological procedures is presently underway. An Australian study could, with considerable advantage, make use of some of the new knowledge these and related studies provide.

In summary then, the aims of a broadly based Australian study of human sexuality should be twofold: first, to develop a methodology and an analytic framework for the study of human sexuality in the Australian context in order that both the specific modes of sexual expression and their distribution and patterning can be examined; second, to develop a methodology for the study of human sexual identity and activity and variations in sexuality across social groups and over the life-cycle of an individual so that these matters can also be examined.

While such a study would provide important benchmark data from which policy concerned with sexually transmitted diseases could be developed, a perhaps more important contribution of the study would be its ability to provide an understanding of the nature and extent of human sexuality in the Australian context.

It is not possible to sketch out the study design in any detail, but a few general comments may be provided.

Sample design

In order to accommodate the research interests of those engaged in the study, a large (of the order of 5000–7000 persons), representative national sample is desirable.

However, a number of issues would need to be clarified before a final decision was made.

- What age range will be considered? Is a minimum age of eighteen appropriate, or should this be lowered to fourteen or fifteen?
- Are there strategic groups within the community which should be over-sampled?
- Should a national survey be supplemented with in-depth studies of particular groups?
- How important is ethnicity for such a study?

Clearly these and related issues are critical for the overall research program. They would need to be fully canvassed in the early stages of any project.

Construction of research instruments

Great care will be needed in the construction of research instruments. These will include, of course, standard socio-demographic items, a variety of relevant socio-psychological measures as well as a range of open and more structured questions dealing with an extensive range of sexually related issues. Recourse will be had to the literature and the use of established scales with proven validity and reliability. The WHO Global Programme on AIDS will clearly be an invaluable source of information. Questionnaires, interview schedules and diaries should be developed in a complementary manner, not only to extend the range of information collected but also to provide additional assessments of reliability and validity.

Methods of data collection

Consideration will need to be given to alternative methods of data collection and the possibility of using a combination of methods. Briefly, there appear to be four alternatives:

- face-to-face interviews;
- self-completed questionnaires;
- telephone interviews;
- the use of diaries.

Standard practice would suggest considerable reliance on

face-to-face interviews and these will very probably provide an important source of data. However, recent work cited previously has pointed to the value of diaries as an important data source. Their use would need to be explored and trials conducted in the pilot stages of any study.

Telephone interviewing is becoming increasingly common. Developing techniques such as CATI (Computer Assisted Telephone Interviewing) allow for the rapid compilation of data. Perhaps the sensitive nature of the data of the proposed research might preclude such an approach, but it should not be dismissed out of hand because of recent research which suggests that the perceived anonymity of telephone interviews prompts respondents to greater frankness than they would display in face-to-face situations.

In the development of the research a great deal of time will need to be devoted to testing the feasibility of different methods of data collection as well as the feasibility of particular research instruments. The cost-effectiveness of different sampling designs associated with different methods of data collection should be determined.

Data analysis

One of the weaknesses of much of the research on human sexuality in the past has been its lack of analytic depth. While it is clearly important to document the range and frequency of the different sexual practices within the community, it is equally important to identify the social and other conditions that give rise to and sustain them. These important matters would obviously need to be addressed during the process of data collection.

The procedures employed during data analysis should also enable causal sequences to be identified and, in this way, provide an analytic depth which other studies have lacked.

A number of relatively new multivariate procedures are available in this connection. These range all the way from the well-established procedures of path analysis based on ordinary least squares and two-stage multiple regression and Lisrel based on confirmatory factor analysis and multiple regression, to various modelling procedures based on log-linear analysis.

CONCLUSION

This chapter has dealt with a major issue in Australian or, for that matter, any society, namely the question of human sexuality. I have argued that, in any systematic sense, little is known about human sexuality in the Australian context. The existence of the HIV epidemic and a variety of other sexually transmitted diseases is clearly one important reason for undertaking such a study at the present time. Equally important is the fact of the centrality of sexuality in human life and our limited understanding of its nature and social patterning.

REFERENCES

Chapters citing these references are listed in square brackets at the end of each entry.

Abramson, P. R. 1990a, 'Sexual science: emerging discipline or oxymoron?', *The Journal of Sex Research*, 27(2), 147–66. [1]

Abramson, P. R. 1990b, 'A brief pause: 25 years of The Journal of Sex Research', *The Journal of Sex Research*, 27(4), 471–2. [1]

Aggleton, P., Davies, P. and Hart, G. (eds) 1990, *AIDS: Individual, Cultural and Policy Dimensions*, London, Falmer Press. [2]

Albury, R. 1990, 'Sexual politics in the 1990s', *Social Alternatives*, 1, 42–6. [2]

Allen, J. A. 1986, 'Evidence and Silence: Feminism and the Limits of History', in *Feminist Challenges*, eds C. Pateman and E. Gross, Sydney, Allen and Unwin, 173–89. [1]

Allen, J. A. 1988, ' "Our Deeply Degraded Sex" and "The Animal in Man": Rose Scott, feminism and sexuality 1890–1920', *Australian Feminist Studies*, 7/8, Summer, 65–94. [1]

Allen, J. A. 1989, 'From Women's History to a History of the Sexes' in *Australian Studies: A Survey*, ed. J. Walter, Melbourne, Oxford University Press, 220–41. [1]

Allen, J. A. 1990a, 'Does Feminism Need a Theory of "The State"?' in *Playing the State: Australian Feminist Interventions*, ed. S. Watson, London, Verso, 21–38. [1, 5]

Allen, J. A. 1990b, *Sex and Secrets: Crimes Involving Australian Women Since 1880*, Melbourne, Oxford University Press. [1, 3, 4]

Allen, J. A. 1991a, 'Contextualizing late nineteenth century feminism: problems and comparisons', *Journal of the Canadian Historical Association*, 1(1), 17–36. [1]

References

Allen, J. A. 1991b, Feminist Critiques of Knowledges: Spatial Anxiety in a Provisional Phase? Paper presented at the Academy of the Humanities Symposium: Beyond the Disciplines, Australian National University, Canberra, 13–15 November. [1]

Allen, J. A. and Reekie, G. R. 1991, Beyond Region: Sexual Patternings in Australian Population History. Paper presented at the Conference of the Australian Historical Association, Darwin, 30 June. [1]

Altman, D. 1972, *Homosexual: Oppression and Liberation*, Sydney, Angus and Robertson. [3]

Altman, D. 1982, *The Homosexualization of America*, Boston, Beacon Press. [1, 2, 5]

Altman, D. 1985, 'Report from the sexual trenches', *Outrage*, 28, September, 16–17. [2]

Altman, D. 1986, *AIDS and the New Puritanism*, London, Pluto Press. [1, 2]

Altman, D. 1989, 'The Emergence of Gay Identity in the USA and Australia', in *Politics of the Future: The Rise of Modern Social Movements*, eds C. Jennett and R. Stewart, Melbourne, Macmillan, 30–55. [2]

Altman, D. 1991, 'The Most Political of Diseases', in *AIDS in Context*, eds V. Minichiello, E. Timewell and D. Plummer, Sydney, Prentice-Hall, 61–76. [2]

Altman, D. et al. 1989, *Homosexuality, Which Homosexuality? International Conference on Gay and Lesbian Studies*, London, GMP and Amsterdam, Uitgeverij An Dekker/Schorer. [5]

Andreski, S. 1989, *Syphilis, Puritanism and Witchhunts: Historical Explorations in the Light of Medicine and Psychoanalysis with a Forecast about AIDS*, Basingstoke, Macmillan. [5]

Araji, S. and Finkelhor, D. 1986, 'Abusers: A Review of the Research', in *A Sourcebook on Child Sexual Abuse*, eds D. Finkelhor and S. Araji, Beverly Hills, Calif., Sage Publications, 119–42. [7]

Archpoet. 1952 [c. 1160] 'Confessio', in *Medieval Latin Lyrics*, ed. H. Waddell, Harmondsworth, Penguin, 182–95. [3]

Arditti, R., Klein, R. D. and Minden, S. (eds) 1984, *Test-tube Women: What Future for Motherhood?*, London, Pandora. [7]

Areskig, B., Uddenberg, N. and Kjessler, B. 1983, 'Background factors in pregnant women with and without fear of childbirth', *Journal of Psychosomatic Obstetrics and Gynaecology*, 2(2), 102–8. [7]

Augustine. 1945 [426], *The City of God*, London, J. M. Dent and Sons. [3]

Ballard, J. A. 1987, 'Ethnicity as a Mask of Confrontation', in *Three Worlds of Inequality: Race, Class and Gender*, eds R. G. Stewart and C. Jennett, South Melbourne, Macmillan, 128–34. [5]

References

Ballard, J. A. 1988, 'Alternatives to the Traditional Public Health Approach', in Commonwealth of Australia, *Living with AIDS: Toward the Year 2000: Report of the Third National Conference on AIDS*, Canberra, Australian Government Publishing Service, 645–8. [5]

Ballard, J. A. 1989, 'The Politics of AIDS', in *The Politics of Health: The Australian Experience*, ed. H. Gardner, Melbourne, Churchill Livingstone, 349–75. [5]

Bardwick, J. 1971, *Psychology of Women: A study of bio-cultural conflicts*, New York, Harper and Row. [4]

Baron, L. 1990, 'Pornography and gender equality: an empirical analysis', *The Journal of Sex Research*, 27(3), 363–80. [1]

Barrett, M. 1980, *Women's Oppression Today*, London, Verso. [1]

Battersby, C. 1989, *Gender and Genius: Towards a Feminist Aesthetics*, London, Women's Press. [4]

Becker, J. V., Skinner, L. J., Abel, G. G. and Tracey, E. C. 1982, 'Incidence and types of sexual dysfunctions in rape and incest victims', *Journal of Sex and Marital Therapy*, 8(1), 65–74. [7]

Bem, S. 1974, 'The measurement of psychological androgyny', *Journal of Consulting and Clinical Psychology*, 42(2), 155–62. [4]

Benjamin, J. 1986, 'An Intersubjectivity of One's Own', in *Feminist Studies/Critical Studies*, ed. T. de Lauretis, Bloomington, Indiana University Press, 78–101. [1]

Benjamin, J. 1988, *The Bonds of Love: Psychoanalysis, Feminism and the Problem of Domination*, New York, Pantheon. [1]

Berg, R. 1986, 'Sexuality: Why Do Women Come Off Second Best?', in *Australian Women: New Feminist Perspectives*, eds N. Grieve and A. Burns, Melbourne, Oxford University Press, 155–70. [1]

Bergstrom-Walen, T. and Nielsen, H. N. 1990, 'Sexual expression among 60–80 year old men and women: a sample from Stockholm, Sweden', *The Journal of Sex Research*, 27(2), 289–96. [1]

Bersani, L. 1988, 'Is the Rectum a Grave?', in *AIDS: Cultural Analysis, Cultural Activism*, ed. D. Crimp, Cambridge, Mass., MIT Press, 197–222. [3, 6]

Bisset, A. 1979, *Black Roots White Flowers. A History of Jazz in Australia*, Sydney, Golden Press. [6]

Bolin, A. 1988, *In Search of Eve: Transsexual Rights of Passage*, Massachusetts, Bergin and Garvey. [3]

Braidotti, R. 1989, 'The Politics of Ontological Difference', in *Between Feminism and Psychoanalysis*, ed. T. Brennan, London, Routledge, 89–105. [4]

Bray, A. 1982, *Homosexuality in Renaissance England*, London, Gay Men's Press. [3]

References

Brecher, E. M. 1969, *The Sex Researchers*, Boston, Little, Brown. [7]

Bretschneider, J. G. and McCoy, N. L. 1988, 'Sexual interest and behavior in healthy 80 to 102 year olds', *Archives of Sexual Behavior*, 17(2), 109–30. [1]

Brod, H. 1990, 'Pornography and the Alienation of Male Sexuality', in *Men, Masculinities and Social Theory*, eds J. Hearn and D. Morgan, London, Unwin Hyman, 124–37. [1]

Brown, B. 1973, *Marx, Freud, and the Critique of Everyday Life*, New York, Monthly Review Press. [4]

Brown, N. O. 1970, *Life Against Death: The Psychoanalytical Meaning of History*, Middleton, Conn., Wesleyan University Press. [4]

Brownmiller, S. 1976, *Against Our Will: Men, Women and Rape*, Harmondsworth, Penguin. [1]

Brumby, M. 1983, 'Australian community attitudes to in-vitro fertilization', *Medical Journal of Australia*, 2(12), 650–3. [7]

Brunt, R. 1982, 'An Immense Verbosity: Permissive Sexual Advice in the 1970s', in *Feminism, Culture and Politics*, eds R. Brunt and C. Rowan, London, Lawrence and Wishart, 143–70. [1]

Bulbeck, C. 1987, *One World Women's Movement*, London, Pluto. [1]

Burgin, V., Donald, J. and Kaplan, C. 1986, *Formations of Fantasy*, London, Methuen. [3]

Butler, J. 1990a, 'Gender Trouble', in *Feminism/Postmodernism*, ed. L. J. Nicholson, New York, Routledge, 324–40. [1]

Butler, J. 1990b, *Gender Trouble: Feminism and the Subversion of Identity*, London, Routledge and Kegan Paul. [1, 4]

Butlin, N. G. 1983, *Our Original Aggression: Aboriginal Populations of Southeastern Australia*, Sydney, Allen and Unwin. [6]

Bynum, C. W. 1987, *Fasting Women: Holy Feast and Holy Fast: The Religious Significance of Food to Medieval Women*, Berkeley, Calif., University of California Press. [1]

Caine, B. 1988, 'Millicent Garrett Fawcett: A Liberal Feminist?', in *Crossing Boundaries: Feminisms and the Critique of Knowledge*, eds B. Caine, E. A. Grosz and M. de Lepervanche, Sydney, Allen and Unwin, 166–79. [1]

Callan, V. J. and Wilks, J. 1982, 'Family size intentions and attitudes to contraception: Australian and Papua New Guinean high school youth', *Australian Journal of Sex Marriage and the Family*, 3(2), 89–94. [7]

Carballo, M., Cleland, J., Carael, M. and Albrecht, G. 1989, 'Research agenda: a cross-national study of patterns of sexual behavior', *The Journal of Sex Research*, 26(3), 287–99. [2]

Carr, A. 1990, 'Reforms which take us backwards', *Outrage*, 80, January, 12. [2]

References

Carter, E. and Watney, S. (eds) 1989, *Taking Liberties*, London, Serpent's Tail. [2]

Castiglia, C. 1990, 'Rebel Without a Closet', in *Engendering Men: The Question of Male Feminist Criticism*, eds J. A. Boone and M. Cadden, New York, Routledge, 207–24. [1]

Castle, Mr and Mrs V. 1914, *Modern Dancing*, New York, Harper and Brothers. [6]

Celemajer, D. 1987, 'Submission or rebellion: anorexia and the body', *Australian Feminist Studies*, 5, Summer, 57–70. [1]

Chafetz, J. S. 1974, *Masculine/Feminine or Human? An Overview of the Sociology of Sex Roles*, Itasha, Ill., Peacock Publications. [4]

Chapman, S. and Hodgson, J. 1988, 'Showers in raincoats: attitudinal barriers to condom use in high-risk heterosexuals', *Community Health Studies*, 12(1), 97–105. [2, 7]

Cixous, H. 1980, 'The laugh of the Medusa', in *New French Feminism: An Anthology*, eds E. Marks and I. de Courtivron, Amherst, University of Massachusetts Press, 245–64. [4]

Cockburn, C. 1983, *Brothers*, London, Pluto Press. [4]

Coleman, A. 1990, 'Expanding the boundaries of sex research', *The Journal of Sex Research*, 27(4), 473–80. [1]

Coleridge, S. T. 1817, *Biographia Literaria*, vol. II, London, Rest Tenner. [6]

Collins, J. K. and Harper, J. 1985, 'Sexual behaviour and peer pressure in adolescent girls', *Australian Journal of Sex, Marriage and Family*, 6(3), 137–42. [7]

Collins, J. K. and Robinson, L. 1986, 'The contraceptive knowledge, attitudes and practice of unmarried adolescents'. *Australian Journal of Sex, Marriage and Family*, 7(3), 132–52. [7]

Commonwealth Department of Community Services and Health 1988, *Benchmark Survey 1986–87, Summary Report: General Population and Adolescents*, Canberra, Australian Government Publishing Service. [7]

Commonwealth of Australia 1988, *AIDS: A Time to Care, A Time to Act. Towards a strategy for Australians*, Canberra, Australian Government Publishing Service. [5]

Commonwealth of Australia 1989, *National HIV/AIDS Strategy. A Policy Information Paper*, Canberra, Australian Government Publishing Service. [5]

Connell, R. W. 1979, 'The concept of role and what to do with it', *Australian and New Zealand Journal of Sociology*, 15(3), 7–17. [3]

Connell, R. W. 1987, *Gender and Power*, Sydney, Allen and Unwin. [3, 4, 7]

References

Connell, R. W. 1990, 'The state, gender, and sexual politics', *Theory and Society*, 19(5), 507–44. [5]

Connell, R. W., Crawford, J., Kippax, S., Dowsett, G. W., Baxter, D., Watson, L. and Berg, R. 1989, 'Facing the epidemic: changes in the sexual lives of gay and bisexual men in Australia and their implications for AIDS prevention strategies', *Social Problems*, 36(4), 384–402. [2]

Connell, R. W. and Kippax, S. 1990, 'Sexuality and the AIDS crisis: patterns of pleasure and practice in an Australian sample of gay and bisexual men', *The Journal of Sex Research*, 27(2), 167–98. [1, 2, 3]

Coward, R. 1984, *Female Desire*, London, Paladin. [3]

Coxon, T. 1988, 'Something sensational . . . the sexual diary as a tool for mapping detailed sexual behaviour', *Sociological Review*, 36(2), 353–67. [7]

Crimp, D. (ed.) 1988, *AIDS: Cultural Analysis, Cultural Activism*, Cambridge, Mass., MIT Press. [2]

Cummins, M. 1971, 'Police and Petting: Informal enforcement of sexual standards', in *Studies in the Sociology of Sex*, ed. J. M. Henslin, New York, Appleton-Century-Crofts, Educational Division, Meredith Corporation, 225–41. [7]

Daly, M. 1978, *Gyn/Ecology: The Metaethics of Radical Feminism*, Boston, Beacon Press. [4]

Davies, P. 1989/90, 'Using personal interviews with diary-keeping to provide improved measures of sexual behavior', *Joint Centre for Survey Methods Newsletter*, 10(1), 8–9. [7]

Davies, P. 1990, 'Patterns in Homosexual Relations: The Use of the Diary Method', *Project SIGMA Working Paper No. 17*, Cardiff, University College, Social Research Unit, 2nd edn. [3]

Davies, P. and Project SIGMA 1992, 'On Relapse: Recidivism or Rational Response', in *AIDS: Rights, Risk and Reason*, eds P. Aggleton, P. Davies and G. Hart, London, Falmer Press. [2]

Davis, K. 1990, 'Sydney march to stem the tide of hate crimes', *Gayzette*, 73, April, 2. [6]

Day, B. 1972, *Sexual Life between Blacks and Whites*, New York, World Publishing. [7]

de Beauvoir, S. 1953, *The Second Sex*, trans. H. M. Parshley, Harmondsworth, Penguin. [4]

de Lauretis, T. 1986, *Feminist Studies/Critical Studies*, Bloomington, Indiana University Press. [4]

de Lauretis, T. 1989a, *Technologies of Gender*, Bloomington, Indiana University Press. [4]

de Lauretis, T. 1989b, 'The essence of the triangle or taking the risk of essentialism seriously: feminist theory in Italy, the U.S. and Britain', *Differences: A Journal of Feminist Cultural Studies*, 1(2), 3–37. [1, 4]

de Lauretis, T. 1990a, 'Upping the Anti [sic] in Feminist Theory', in *Conflicts in Feminism*, eds M. Hirsch and E. F. Keller, New York, Routledge, 255–70. [1]

de Lauretis, T. 1990b, 'Eccentric subjects: feminist theory and feminist consciousness', *Feminist Studies*, 16(2), 115–50. [1]

de Sade, Marquis 1785, '120 Days of Sodom', in *The Marquis de Sade. The 120 Days of Sodom and other writings*, comp. A. Wainhouse and R. Seaver, 1966, New York, Grove, 183–674. [3]

DeLamater, J. and MacCorqodale, P. 1979, *Premarital Sexuality*, Madison, Wisconsin, University of Wisconsin Press. [7]

D'Emilio, J. 1983, 'Capitalism and Gay Identity', in *Powers of Desire: The Politics of Sexuality*, eds A. Snitow, C. Stansell and S. Thompson, New York, Monthly Review Press, 140–52. [5]

Diamond, I. and Quinby, L. (eds) 1988, *Feminism and Foucault: Reflections on Resistance*, Boston, Northeastern University Press. [1]

Dinnerstein, D. 1976, *The Mermaid and the Minotaur*, New York, Harper and Row. [3]

Dixson, M. 1976, *The Real Matilda: Women and Identity in Australia 1788–1975*, Ringwood, Vic., Penguin. [1]

Donzelot, J. 1979, *The Policing of Families*, New York, Pantheon. [4]

Dowsett, G. W. 1990, 'Reaching men who have sex with men in Australia. An overview of AIDS education: community intervention and community attachment strategies', *Australian Journal of Social Issues*, 25(3) 186–98. [3]

Duberman, M. B., Vicinus, M. and Chauncey Jr, G. (eds) 1989, *Hidden from History: Reclaiming the Gay and Lesbian Past*, New York, New American Library. [5]

DuBois, E. 1991, 'Eleanor Flexner and the history of American feminism,' *Gender and History*, 3(1), 81–90. [6]

Dunstan, K, 1968, *Wowsers*, Sydney, Angus and Robertson. [6]

Easlea, B. 1981, *Science and Sexual Oppression*, London, Weidenfeld and Nicholson. [1]

Edwards, A. 1989, 'The sex/gender distinction: has it outlived its usefulness?', *Australian Feminist Studies*, 10, Summer, 1–12. [1]

Edwards, T. 1990, 'Beyond sex and gender: masculinity, homosexuality and social theory', in *Men, Masculinities and Social Theory*, eds J. Hearn and D. Morgan, London, Unwin Hyman, 110–23. [4]

Eisenstein, H. and Jardine, A. (eds) 1980, *The Future of Difference*, Boston, G. K. Hall. [3]

References

Ellis, B. J. and Symons, D. 1990, 'Sex differences in sexual fantasy: an evolutionary psychological approach', *The Journal of Sex Research*, 27(4), 527–55. [1]

Ellis, H. 1923 [1897], *Studies in the Psychology of Sex, Vol. 2: Sexual Inversion*, Philadelphia, Davis. [3]

Epstein, C. F. 1988, *Deceptive Distinctions: sex, gender, and the social order*, New Haven, Yale University Press. [3]

Epstein, S. 1987, 'Gay politics, ethnic identity: the limits of social constructionism', *Socialist Review*, 17(3/4), 9–54. [2]

Faderman, L. 1991, *Odd Girls and Twilight Lovers: A History of Lesbian Life in Twentieth Century America*, New York, Columbia University Press. [1]

Field, J. and Wadsworth, J. 1989/90, 'Developing the methodology for a national survey of sexual attitudes and lifestyles', *Joint Centre for Survey Methods Newsletter*, 10(1), 5–8. [7]

Foucault, M. 1973a, *Madness and Civilization: a history of insanity in the age of reason*, trans. R. Howard, New York, Vintage Books. [3]

Foucault, M. 1973b, *The Birth of the Clinic*, trans. A. Sheridan, New York, Pantheon. [3]

Foucault, M. 1977, *Discipline and Punish*, trans. A. Sheridan, New York, Pantheon. [3]

Foucault, M. 1978, *The History of Sexuality, Vol. 1: An Introduction*, trans. R. Hurley, Harmondsworth, Penguin. [3, 4, 5]

Fraser, N. 1989, *Unruly Practices: Power, Discourse and Gender in Contemporary Social Theory*, Minneapolis, University of Minnesota Press. [1]

Fraser, S. E. and Fraser, B. J. 1982, 'Australian attitudes towards abortion: recent complementary surveys', *Australian Journal of Sex, Marriage and Family*, 3(4), 171–80. [7]

Freccero, C. 1990, 'Notes of a Post-Sex War Theorizer', in *Conflicts in Feminism*, eds M. Hirsch and E. F. Keller, New York, Routledge, 305–25. [1]

Freedman, E. B. and D'Emilio, J. 1988, *Intimate Matters: A History of Sexuality in America*, New York, Harper and Row. [5]

Freedman, E. B. and D'Emilio, J. 1990, 'Problems encountered in writing the history of sexuality', *The Journal of Sex Research*, 27(4), 481–96. [1]

Freud, S. 1953 [1900], 'The Interpretation of Dreams', in *Complete Psychological Works*, standard edn, vols 4 and 5, London, Hogarth. [3]

Freud, S. 1953 [1905], 'Three Essays on the Theory of Sexuality', in *Complete Psychological Works*, standard edn, vol. 7, London, Hogarth. [3]

References

Freud, S. 1963 [1930], *'Civilization and its Discontents*, trans. J. Riviere, rev. J. Strachey, London, Hogarth. [3]

Freund, K. and Watson, R. 1990, 'Mapping the boundaries of courtship disorder', *The Journal of Sex Research*, 27(4), 589–606. [1]

Fritz, G. S., Stoll, K. and Wagner, N. N. 1981, 'A comparison of males and females who were sexually molested as children', *Journal of Sex and Marital Therapy*, 7(1), 54–9. [7]

Frye, M. 1983, *The Politics of Reality: Essays in Feminist Theory*, Trumansburg, NY, The Crossing Press. [1]

Fuss, D. 1989, *Essentially Speaking: Feminism, Nature and Difference*, New York, Routledge. [1, 4]

Gagnon, J. H. 1965, 'Female child victims of sex offenses', *Social Problems*, 13(2), 176–92. [7]

Gagnon, J. H. 1975, 'Sex research and social change', *Archives of Sexual Behavior*, 4(2), 111–41. [7]

Gagnon, J. H. 1988, 'Sex research and sexual conduct in the era of AIDS', *Journal of Acquired Immune Deficiency Syndrome*, 1(6), 593–601. [2]

Gagnon, J. H. and Simon, W. 1974, *Sexual Conduct: The Social Sources of Human Sexuality*, London, Hutchinson. [3, 4]

Game, A. and Pringle, R. 1979, 'Sexuality and the suburban dream', *Australian and New Zealand Journal of Sociology*, 15(2), 4–15. [3, 4]

Game, A. and Pringle, R. 1983, *Gender at Work*, Sydney, Allen and Unwin. [4]

Garner, S. N. 1989, 'Feminism, Psychoanalysis and the Heterosexual Imperative', in *Feminism and Psychoanalysis*, eds R. Feldstein and J. Roof, Ithaca, NY, Cornell University Press, 164–81. [1]

Gatens, M. 1983, 'A Critique of the Sex/Gender Distinction', in *Beyond Marxism? Interventions After Marx*, eds J. A. Allen and P. Patton, Sydney, Intervention Publications, 143–60. [1, 4]

Gatens, M. 1989, 'Woman and her double(s): sex, gender and ethics', *Australian Feminist Studies*, 10, Summer, 33–47. [1]

Gatens, M. 1991, *Feminism and Philosophy*, Bloomington, Indiana University Press. [1]

Giddens, A. 1984, *The Constitution of Society*, Cambridge, Polity Press. [3]

Glassner, B. 1988, *Bodies: Why We Look the Way We Do (And How We Feel About It)*, New York, Putnam. [3]

Goddard, M. 1991, 'Blood sport: killing queers', *Outrage*, 95, April, 16–21. [2]

References

Goggin, M. and Hee, A. 1990, 'Say yes to reaching out', *National AIDS Bulletin*, 4(9), 17–18. [2]

Goldman, R. J. and Goldman, J. 1984, 'Perceptions of sexual experience in childhood: relating normal development to incest', *Australian Journal of Sex, Marriage and Family*, 5(3), 159–66. [7]

Goldman, R. J. and Goldman, J. 1988, 'The prevalence and nature of child sexual abuse in Australia', *Australian Journal of Sex, Marriage and Family*, 9(2), 94–106. [7]

Gordon, L. 1986, 'What's New in Women's History', in *Feminist Studies/Critical Studies*, ed. T. de Lauretis, Bloomington, Indiana University Press, 20–30. [4]

Gordon, P. (unpub.), Safe Sex Education Workshops for Gay and Bisexual Men. A Review, London. [4]

Gosselin, C. and Wilson, G. 1980, *Sexual Variations: Fetishism, Sadomasochism and Transvestism*, New York, Simon and Schuster. [7]

Graff, G. 1989, 'Co-optation', in *The New Historicism*, ed. H. A. Veeser, New York, Routledge, Chapman and Hall, 168–81. [5]

Greenberg, D. F. 1988, *The Construction of Homosexuality*, Chicago, University of Chicago Press. [3]

Gross, L. 1991, 'Out of the mainstream: sexual minorities and the mass media', *Journal of Homosexuality*, 21(1/2), 19–46. [1]

Grosz, E. 1987, 'Towards a corporeal feminism', *Australian Feminist Studies*, 7, Summer, 1–16. [1]

Grosz, E. 1988, 'The In(ter)vention of Feminist Knowledges', in *Crossing Boundaries: Feminisms and the Critique of Knowledge*, eds B. Caine, E. A. Grosz and M. de Lepervanche, Sydney, Allen and Unwin, 92–104. [1]

Grosz, E. 1989, *Sexual Subversions: Three French Feminists*, Sydney, Allen and Unwin. [1]

Grosz, E. 1990a, *Jacques Lacan: A Feminist Introduction*, London, Routledge. [1]

Grosz, E. 1990b, 'A Note on Essentialism and Difference', in *Feminist Knowledge: Critique and Construct*, ed. S. Gunew, London, Routledge, 332–45. [1]

Grosz, E. 1991, Feminism and Theories of the Body. Paper presented at the Australian Women's Studies Association Conference, Brisbane, 30 November–2 December. [1]

Gutek, B. A. 1989, 'Sexuality in the Workplace: Key Issues in Social Research and Organizational Practice', in *The Sexuality of Organization*, eds J. Hearn, D. L. Sheppard, P. Tancred-Sheriff and G. Burrell, London, Sage, 56–70. [4]

References

Hall, S. 1980, 'Reformism and the Legislation of Consent', in *Permissiveness and Control: The Fate of the Sixties Legislation*, National Deviancy Conference, London, Macmillan, 1–44. [5]

Halperin, D. M. 1990, *One Hundred Years of Homosexuality and Other Essays on Greek Love*, New York, Routledge. [5]

Hansen, C. E. and Evans, A. 1985, 'Bisexuality reconsidered: an idea in pursuit of a definition', *Journal of Homosexuality*, 11(1/2), 1–6. [7]

Harding, S. 1991, *Whose Science? Whose Knowledge? Thinking From Women's Lives*, Ithaca, NY, Cornell University Press. [1]

Hearn, J. and Parkin, W. 1987, *'Sex' at 'Work': The Power and Paradox of Organization Sexuality*, Brighton, Wheatsheaf Books. [3, 4]

Hearn, J., Sheppard, D. L., Tancred-Sheriff, P. and Burrell, G. (eds) 1989, *The Sexuality of Organization*, London, Sage. [4]

Heiman, J. R., Rowland, D. L., Hatch, J. P. and Gladve, B. A. 1991, 'Psychophysiological and endrocrine responses to sexual arousal in women', *Archives of Sexual Behavior*, 20(2), 171–86. [1]

Hendrick, S. and Hendrick, C. 1987, 'Multidimensionality of sexual attitudes', *The Journal of Sex Research*, 23(4), 502–26. [7]

Henslin, J. M. 1971, 'The Sociological Point of View', in *Studies in the Sociology of Sex*, ed. J. M. Henslin, New York, Appleton-Century-Crofts, 1–6. [7]

Herdt, G. 1981, *Guardians of the Flutes*, New York, McGraw-Hill. [3]

Herdt, G. (ed.) 1984, *Ritualized Homosexuality in Melanesia*, Berkeley, University of California Press. [3]

Herek, G. 1989, 'Hate crimes against lesbians and gay men', *American Psychologist*, 44(6), 948–55. [2]

Hite, S. 1977, *The Hite Report: A Nationwide Study on Female Sexuality*, Sydney, Summit Books/Paul Hamlyn. [4]

Hollway, W. 1984, 'Gender Difference and the Production of Subjectivity', in *Changing the Subject: Psychology, Social Regulation and Subjectivity*, eds J. Henriques, W. Hollway, C. Urwin, C. Venn and V. Walkerdine, London, Methuen, 227–63. [4]

Hong, S.-M. 1983, 'Sex, religion and factor analytically derived attitudes towards homosexuality', *Australian Journal of Sex, Marriage and Family*, 4(3), 142–50. [7]

Hong, S.-M. 1985, 'Sexual permissiveness—a comparison between general public and college-students', *Australian Psychologist*, 20(1), 85–6. [7]

Horn, J. and Chetwynd, J. 1989, *Changing sexual practices amongst homosexual men in response to AIDS*, Report to the New Zealand Department of Health, September. [2]

References

Hornibrook, F. A. n.d. [1935], *Without Reserve*, London, Heinemann. [6]

Humphries, M. 1985, 'Gay machismo', in *The Sexuality of Men*, eds A. Metcalf and M. Humphries, London, Pluto, 70–85. [4]

Irigaray, L. 1985, *This Sex Which Is Not One*, Ithaca, NY, Cornell University Press. [4]

Irvine, J. M. 1990a, *Disorders of Desire: Sex and Gender in Modern American Sexology*, Philadelphia, Temple University Press. [1]

Irvine, J. M. 1990b, 'From difference to sameness: gender and ideology in sexual science', *The Journal of Sex Research*, 27(1), 7–24. [1]

Jackson, P. 1989, *Male Homosexuality in Thailand*, New York, Global Academic Publishers. [2]

Jeffreys, S. 1985, *The Spinster and Her Enemies: Feminism and Sexuality 1880–1930*, London, Pandora. [1]

Jeffreys, S. 1990, *Anti-Climax: The Sexual Revolution Reconsidered*, London, The Women's Press. [1]

Johnston, C. 1981, 'Review of M. Mieli, "Homosexuality and Liberation"', *Gay Information*, 5, 20–1. [3]

Julian, E. and Over, R. 1988, 'Male sexual arousal across five modes of erotic stimulation', *Archives of Sexual Behavior*, 17(2), 131–43. [1]

Kaplan, E. 1989, 'Can bad models suggest good policies? sexual mixing and the AIDS epidemic', *The Journal of Sex Research*, 26(3), 301–14. [2]

Kappeler, S. 1987, *The Pornography of Representation*, Cambridge, Polity Press. [1]

Keat, R. 1986, 'The human body in social theory: Reich, Foucault and the repressive hypothesis', *Radical Philosophy*, 42, 24–32. [3]

Keller, E. F. 1985, *Reflections on Gender and Science*, New Haven, Yale University Press. [1]

Kent, S. K. 1987, *Sex and Suffrage in Britain 1860–1914*, Princeton, Princeton University Press. [6]

Kessler, S. J. and McKenna, W. 1978, *Gender: An Ethnomethodological Approach*, New York, Wiley. [3]

King, K. 1990, 'Producing Sex, Theory and Culture: Gay/Straight Remappings in Contemporary Feminism', in *Conflicts in Feminism*, eds M. Hirsch and E. F. Keller, New York, Routledge, 82–101. [1]

Kingston, B. R. 1986, 'The Lady and the Australian Girl: Some Thoughts on Nationalism and Class', in *Australian Women*, eds N. Grieve and A. Burns, Melbourne, Oxford University Press, 27–41. [1]

References

Kinsey, A. C., Pomeroy, W. B. and Martin, C. E. 1948 *Sexual Behavior in the Human Male*, Philadelphia, Saunders. [4]

Kinsey, A. C., Pomeroy, W. B., Martin, C. E. and Gebhard, P. H. 1953, *Sexual Behavior in the Human Female*, Philadelphia, Saunders. [4, 7]

Kinsman, G. 1987, *The Regulation of Desire: Sexuality in Canada*, Montreal, Black Rose. [5]

Kippax, S., Crawford, J., Dowsett, G. W., Bond, G., Sinnott, V., Baxter, D., Berg, R., Connell, R. W. and Watson, L. 1990, 'Gay men's knowledge of HIV transmission and "safe sex": a question of accuracy', *Australian Journal of Social Issues*, 25(3), 199–219. [7]

Kippax, S., Crawford, J., Waldby, C. and Benton, P. 1990, 'Women negotiating heterosex: implications for AIDS prevention', *Women's Studies International Forum*, 13(6), 533–42. [2, 3]

Klein, F., Sepekoff, B. and Wolf, T. J. 1985, 'Sexual orientation: a multi-variable dynamic process', *Journal of Homosexuality*, 11(1/2), 35–49. [7]

Klein, F. and Wolf, T. J. (eds) 1985, 'Bisexualities theory and research', *Journal of Homosexuality*, 11(1/2), special double issue. [7]

Koedt, A. 1973, 'Myth of the Vaginal Orgasm', in *Radical Feminism: Notes from the Second Year*, eds E. Levine, A. Rapone and A. Koedt, New York, Quadrangle, 198–207. [4]

Kosik, K. 1976, *Dialectics of the Concrete: a study of the problems of man and world*, Dordrecht, D. Reidel Publishing Company. [3]

Kovacs, G. T., Dunn, K. and Selwood, T. 1986, 'Teenage girls and sex: the Victorian Action Centre Survey', *Australian Journal of Sex, Marriage and Family*, 7(4), 217–34. [7]

Krafft-Ebing, R. von 1965 [1886], *Psychopathia Sexualis*, New York, Paperback Library, 12th edn. [3]

Krishnamoorthy, S., Trlin, A. and Khoo, S.-E. 1983, 'Contraceptive risk-taking among never-married youth', *Australian Journal of Sex, Marriage and Family*, 4(3), 151–7. [7]

Kristeva, J. 1984, *Revolution in Poetic Language*, trans. M. Waller, New York, Columbia University Press. [3]

Kuhn, T. S. 1962, *The Structure of Scientific Revolutions*, Chicago, University of Chicago Press. [3]

Lakatos, I. 1970, 'Falsification and the Methodology of Scientific Research Programmes', in *Criticism and the Growth of Knowledge*, eds I. Lakatos and A. Musgrave, Cambridge, Cambridge University Press, 91–196. [3]

Lake, M. 1986, 'The politics of respectability: identifying the masculinist context', *Historical Studies*, 22(86), 116–31. [1]

References

Langfeldt, T. 1980, 'Aspects of Sexual Development, Problems and Therapy in Children', in *Proceedings of the International Symposium on Childhood and Sexuality*, ed. J. M. Samson, Montreal, Editions Etudes Vivantes. [7]

Lawson, S. 1988, *The Archibald Paradox*, Ringwood, Vic., Penguin. [1]

Lees, S. 1986, *Losing Out, Sexuality and Adolescent Girls*, London, Hutchinson. [6]

Leidholdt, D. and Raymond, J. G. 1990, *The Sexual Liberals and the Attack on Feminism*, New York, Pergamon. [6]

Lester, D. 1975, *Unusual Sexual Behavior*, Springfield Ill., Charles C. Thomas. [3]

Lockhart, W. B. et al. [The Presidential Commission on Obscenity and Pornography] 1970, *The Report of the Commission on Obscenity and Pornography*, Washington DC, US Government Printing Office. [3]

Lyotard, J. 1984, *The Postmodern Condition: A Report on Knowledge*, trans. G. Bennington and B. Massumi, Manchester, Manchester University Press. [3]

McCabe, M. P. 1987, 'Desired and experienced levels of premarital affection and sexual intercourse during dating', *The Journal of Sex Research*, 23(1), 23–33. [7]

McCabe, M. P. and Collins, J. K. 1983, 'The sexual and affectional attitudes and experiences of Australian adolescents during dating: the effects of age, church attendance, type of school and socioeconomic class', *Archives of Sexual Behavior*, 12(6), 525–39. [7]

MacInnes, C. 1973, *Loving Them Both*, London, Martin, Brian and O'Keefe. [7]

McIntosh, M. 1968, 'The homosexual role', *Social Problems*, 16(2), 182–92. [2, 3, 5]

McIntosh, M. 1978, 'Who Needs Prostitutes?: The Ideology of Male Sexual Needs', in *Women, Sexuality and Social Control*, eds C. Smart and B. Smart, London, Routledge and Kegan Paul, 53–64. [1]

McIntosh, M. 1981, 'Postscript: "The homosexual role" revisited', in *The Making of the Modern Homosexual*, ed. K. Plummer, London, Hutchinson, 44–9. [5]

MacKinnon, C. A. 1982, 'Feminism, marxism, method and the state', *Signs*, 7(3), 515–44. [1]

MacKinnon, C. A. 1987, *Feminism Unmodified: Discourses on Life and Law*, Cambridge, Mass., Harvard University Press. [4]

MacKinnon, C. A. 1989, *Toward a Feminist Theory of the State*, Cambridge, Mass., Harvard University Press. [4]

References

McQueen, D. 1989/90, 'The stability and consistency of sensitive information obtained from face-to-face and computer-assisted interviews', *Joint Centre for Survey Methods Newsletter*, 10(1), 9–12. [7]

Magarey, S. 1985, Conditions for the Emergence of an Activist Feminist Movement in Australia in the late Nineteenth Century. Paper to the annual conference of Sociological Association of Australia and New Zealand, Brisbane. [3]

Malinowski, B. 1927, *Sex and Repression in Savage Society*, London, Routledge and Kegan Paul. [3]

Malinowski, B. 1932 [1929], *The Sexual Life of Savages in North-Western Melanesia*, London, Routledge and Kegan Paul, 3rd edn. [3]

Malinowski, B. 1960 [1944], *A Scientific Theory of Culture*, New York, Oxford University Press. [3]

Marbury, E. 1914, 'Introduction', in *Modern Dancing*, Mr and Mrs V. Castle, New York, Harper and Brothers, 19–29. [6]

Marcuse, H. 1955, *Eros and Civilization*, Boston, Beacon Press. [3, 4]

Marcuse, H. 1968, *One Dimensional Man*, London, Sphere Books. [3, 4]

Marshall, D. S. and Suggs, R. C. (eds) 1971, *Human Sexual Behavior: Variations in the Ethnographic Spectrum*, New York, Basic Books. [3]

Marshall, J. 1981, 'Pansies, Perverts and Macho Men: Changing conceptions of male homosexuality', in *The Making of the Modern Homosexual*, ed. K. Plummer, London, Hutchinson, 133–54. [4]

Martin, B. 1988, 'Feminism, Criticism and Foucault', in *Feminism and Foucault: Reflections on Resistance*, eds I. Diamond and L. Quinby, Boston, Northeastern University Press, 3–20. [1]

Martin, E. 1989, *The Woman in the Body: A Cultural Analysis of Reproduction*, Boston, Beacon Press. [1]

Masters, W. H. and Johnson, V. E. 1966, *Human Sexual Response*, Boston, Little, Brown. [3, 4]

Masters, W. H. and Johnson, V. E. 1970, *Homosexuality in Perspective*, Boston, Little, Brown. [3]

Matthews, J. J. 1984, *Good and Mad Women*, Sydney, Allen and Unwin. [4]

Mead, M. 1949, *Male and Female: A study of the sexes in a changing world*, London, Gollancz. [3]

Mead, M. 1963 [1935], *Sex and Temperament in Three Primitive Societies*, New York, Morrow. [3]

Mieli, M. 1980, *Homosexuality and Liberation: Elements of a gay critique*, trans. D. Fernbach, London, Gay Men's Press. [3]

References

Milan, R. J. and Kilman, P. R. 1987, 'Interpersonal factors in premarital contraception', *The Journal of Sex Research*, 23, 289–321. [7]

Millett, K. 1972, *Sexual Politics*, London, Abacus. [3, 4]

Minow, M. 1990, *Making All the Difference: Inclusion, Exclusion, and American Law*, Ithaca, NY, Cornell University Press. [5]

Mitchell, J. 1971, *Woman's Estate*, Harmondsworth, Penguin. [3]

Mitchell, J. 1974, *Psychoanalysis and Feminism: Freud, Reich, Laing and Women*, New York, Vintage Books. [3, 4]

Modjeska, D. 1981, *Exiles at Home: Australian Women Writers 1925–1945*, Sydney, Angus and Robertson. [1]

Moodie, T. D., with Ndatshe, V. and Sibuyi, B. 1989, 'Migrancy and Male Sexuality in the South African Gold Mines', in *Hidden From History: Reclaiming the Gay and Lesbian Past*, eds M. B. Duberman, M. Vicinus and G. Chauncey Jr, New York, New American Library, 411–25. [2]

Mooney, J. 1984, 'AIDS: A special community report', *Women's Day* (Sydney), December 17, 33–5. [2]

Moran, L. 1989, 'Sexual Fix, Sexual Surveillance: Homosexual in Law', in *Coming on Strong: Gay Politics and Culture*, eds S. Shepherd and M. Wallis, London, Unwin Hyman, 180–97. [5]

Morgan, D. H. J. 1990, ' "No More Heroes"?: Masculinity, Violence and the Civilising Process', in *State, Private Life and Political Change*, eds L. Jamieson and H. Corr, London, Macmillan, 13–30. [5]

Mort, F. 1980, 'Sexuality: Regulation and Contestation', in *Homosexuality: Power and Politics*, ed. Gay Left Collective, London, Allison and Busby, 38–51. [5]

Mulligan, T. and Palguta, R. F. 1991, 'Sexual interest, activity and satisfaction among male nursing home residents', *Archives of Sexual Behavior*, 20(2), 199–204. [1]

Neely, C. T. 1989, 'Constructing Female Sexuality in the Renaissance: Stratford, London, Windsor and Vienna', in *Feminism and Psychoanalysis*, eds R. Feldstein and J. Roof, Ithaca, NY, Cornell University Press, 209–29. [1]

Nestle, J. 1987, *A Restricted Country*, Ithaca, NY, Firebrand Books. [1]

O'Carroll, T. 1982, *Paedophilia: The Radical Case*, Boston, Alyson Publications. [1, 3]

Orton, S. and Quick, S. 1989/90, 'Monitoring attitudes and behavior in response to AIDS', *Joint Centre for Survey Methods Newsletter*, 10(1), 3–5. [7]

Oxford English Dictionary 1933, Oxford, Oxford University Press. [1]

References

Padgug, R. 1989, 'Gay Villain, Gay Hero', in *Passion and Power*, eds K. Peiss and C. Simmons, Philadelphia, Temple University Press, 14–21. [2]

Pankhurst, C. 1913, *The Great Scourge and How To End It*, London, David Nutt, 14–21. [6]

Parker, R. 1990, *Bodies, Pleasures and Passions*, Boston, Beacon Press. [2]

Parker, R. G. and Carballo, M. 1990, 'Qualitative research on homosexual and bisexual behavior relevant to HIV/AIDS', *The Journal of Sex Research*, 27(4), 497–525. [1]

Parker, R. G., Guimaraes, C. D., and Struchner, C. D. 1989, The Impact of AIDS Health Promotion for Gay and Bisexual Men in Rio de Janeiro, Brazil. Paper to WHO Workshop on AIDS Health Promotion Activities Directed towards Gay and Bisexual Men, Geneva, May 29–31. [3]

Parnell, B. 1989, 'Peer education: its role in AIDS prevention', *National AIDS Bulletin*, 3(5), 32–7. [2]

Parsons, T. and Bales, R. F. 1956, *Family Socialization and Interaction Process*, London, Routledge. [4]

Pateman, C. 1988, *The Sexual Contract*, Cambridge, Polity Press. [1, 2, 4, 5, 6]

Pateman, C. 1990, 'Sex and Power', *Ethics*, 100, January, 398–407. [4]

Pawlak, A. E., Boulet, J. R. and Bradford, J. M. W. 1991, 'Discriminant analysis of a sexual functioning inventory with intrafamilial and extrafamilial child molesters', *Archives of Sexual Behavior*, 20(1), 27–34. [1]

Perkins, R. 1983, *The 'Drag Queen' Scene: Transsexuals in King's Cross*, Sydney, Allen and Unwin. [3]

Peters, R. 1973, 'The First Kiss', in *The Male Muse: A Gay Anthology*, ed. Ian Young, New York, The Crossing Press, 89. [3]

Peterson, C. C. and Peterson, J. L. 1987, 'Australian students' rating of AIDS relative to other community problems', *Australian Journal of Sex, Marriage and Family*, 8(4), 194–200. [7]

Pinney, E. M., Gerrand, M. and Denney, N. W. 1987, 'The Pinney satisfaction inventory', *The Journal of Sex Research*, 23(2), 233–51. [7]

Plummer, K. 1975, *Sexual Stigma: An Interactionist Account*, London, Routledge and Kegan Paul. [4]

Pollak, M. 1988, *Les homosexuels et le sida: sociologie d'une épidemié*, Paris, Éditions A. M. Métailié. [3]

Pomeroy, W. B. 1972, *Dr, Kinsey and the Institute for Sex Research*. New York, Harper and Row. [3]

References

Pringle, R. 1988, *Secretaries Talk: Sexuality, Power and Work*, Sydney, Allen and Unwin. [1, 3, 4]

Pronger, B. 1990, *The Arena of Masculinity*, New York, St Martin's Press. [2]

Radi, H. (ed.) n.d. [1988], *200 Australian Women. A Redress Anthology*, Sydney, Women's Redress Press. [6]

Raymond, J. 1979, *The Transsexual Empire*, Boston, Beacon Press. [4]

Reich, W. 1969, *The Sexual Revolution*, New York, Farrer, Strauss and Giroux. [4]

Reich, W. 1972, *Sexpol: Essays 1929–1934*, ed. L. Baxandall, New York, Vintage. [3]

Reiche, R. 1974, *Sexuality and Class Relations*, New York, New Left Books. [4]

Reiss, I. L. 1967, *The Social Context of Pre-marital Permissiveness*, New York, Holt, Rinehart and Winston. [7]

Reiss, I. L. 1983, 'Trouble in Paradise: The Current Status of Sexual Science', in *Challenges in Sexual Science*, ed. C. M. Davis, Iowa, Society for the Scientific Study of Sex, 174–90. [7]

Rich, A. 1979, *On Lies, Secrets and Silence*, New York, Norton. [4]

Rich, A. 1980, 'Compulsory heterosexuality and lesbian existence', *Signs*, 5(4), 631–60. [3, 6]

Rich, A. 1986, 'Review essay: feminism and sexuality in the 1980s', *Feminist Studies*, 12(4), 525–61. [1]

Robinson, I. E. and Jedlicka, D. 1982, 'Change in sexual attitudes and behavior of college students from 1965 to 1980: a research note', *Journal of Marriage and the Family*, 44(1), 237–40. [7]

Rosen, A. 1974, *Rise Up, Women! The Militant Campaign of the Women's Social and Political Union 1903–1914*, London, Routledge and Kegan Paul. [6]

Rosen, R. C., Kostis, J. B. and Jekelis, A. W. 1988, 'Beta-blocker effects on sexual function in normal males', *Archives of Sexual Behavior*, 17(3), 241–56. [1]

Rosenthal, D., Moore, S. and Brumen, I. 1990, 'Ethnic group differences in adolescents' responses to AIDS', *Australian Journal of Social Issues*, 25(3), 220–39. [2]

Ross, M. W. 1982, 'Some effects of heterosexual marriage on homosexual desire', *Australian Journal of Sex, Marriage and Family*, 3(1), 25–9. [7]

Rout, E. A. 1925, *Sex and Exercise, A Study of the Sex Function in Women and Its Relation to Exercise*. London, Heinemann. [6]

Royal Commission on the Decline of the Birth-Rate and on the Mortality of Infants in New South Wales 1904, *Report*, Sydney, New South Wales Government Printer. [6]

References

Rubin, G. 1975, 'The traffic in women: notes on the "political economy" of sex', in *Toward an Anthropology of Women*, ed. R. Reiter, New York, Monthly Review Press, 157–210. [3]

Rubin, G. 1979, 'Sexual Politics, the New Right, and the Sexual Fringe', in *What Color is Your Handkerchief? A Lesbian S/M Sexuality Reader*, ed. Samois, Berkeley, Calif., Samois, 28–35. [4]

Rubin, G. 1981, 'The Leather Menace: Comments on Politics and S/M', in *Coming to Power: Writing and Graphics on Lesbian S/M*, ed. Samois, Boston, Alyson Publications, 192–227. [1]

Rubin, L. B. 1976, *Worlds of Pain: Life in the Working Class Family*, New York, Basic Books. [4]

Ryan, P. 1987, 'Soft-core sex', *New Internationalist*, 175, September, 24. [2]

Sargent, D. 1983, 'Reformulating (homo)sexual politics: radical theory and practice in the gay movement', in *Beyond Marxism? Interventions After Marx*, eds J. A. Allen and P. Patton, Sydney, Intervention Publications, 163–82. [3]

Sawicki, J. 1988, 'Identity Politics and Sexual Freedom, Foucault and Feminism', in *Foucault and Feminism*, eds I. Diamond and L. Quinby, Boston, Northeastern University Press, 177–92. [1]

Sawicki, J. 1991, *Disciplining Foucault: Feminism, Power and the Body*, New York, Routledge, Chapman and Hall. [1]

Schaffer, B. B. and Lamb, G. B. 1974, 'Exit, voice and access', *Social Science Information*, 13(6), 73–90. [5]

Schaffer, K. 1989, *Women and the Bush: Forces of desire in the Australian cultural tradition*, Cambridge, Cambridge University Press. [1]

Schiavi, R. C., Derogatis, L. R., Kuriansky, J., O'Connor, D. and Sharpe, L. 1979, 'The assessment of sexual function and marital interaction', *Journal of Sex and Marital Therapy*, 5(3), 169–224. [7]

Schmidt, G. 1990, 'Foreword: the debate on pedophilia', *Journal of Homosexuality* [Special Issue: Male Intergenerational Intimacy: Historical Socio-Psychological and Legal Perspectives], 20 (1/2), 1–4. [1]

Segal, L. 1983, 'Sensual Uncertainty or Why the Clitoris is not Enough', in *Sex and Love: New Thoughts on Old Contradictions*, eds S. Cartledge and J. Ryan, London, The Women's Press, 30–47. [1]

Segal, L. 1987, *Is the Future Female?* London: Virago. [3]

Sgroi, S. M. 1978, 'Child Sexual Assault, Guidelines for Investigation and Assessment', in *Sexual Assault of Children and*

References

Adolescents, eds A. W. Burgess, A. N. Groth, L. L. Holstrom and S. M. Sgroi, Lexington, Mass., Heath, 129–42. [7]

Shapiro, M. J. 1987, 'The Rhetoric of Social Science: The Political Responsibilities of the Scholar', in *The Rhetoric of the Human Sciences*, eds J. Nelson, A. Megill and D. McCloskey, Madison, University of Wisconsin Press, 363–80. [5]

Sheridan, S. 1990, 'Feminist Knowledges, Women's Liberation and Women's Studies', in *Feminist Knowledges*, ed. S. Gunew, London, Routledge, 36–55. [1]

Shilts, R. 1987, *And the Band Played On*, New York, St Martin's Press. [3]

Shorter, E. 1982, *A History of Women's Bodies*, London, Allen Lane. [6]

Showalter, E. 1990, *Sexual Anarchy, Gender and Culture at the Fin de Siecle*. New York, Viking. [6]

Siedlecky, S. and Wyndham, D. 1990, *Populate and Perish, Australian Women's Fight for Birth Control*. Sydney, Allen and Unwin. [6]

Singer, L. 1989, 'Bodies—pleasures—powers', *Differences*, 1(1), Winter, 45–65. [2]

Singer, P. and Wells, D. 1985, *Making Babies: The New Science and Ethics of Conception*, New York, Scribners. [7]

Singh, B. K. 1980, 'Trends in attitudes to premarital sexual relations', *Journal of Marriage and the Family*, 42(2), 387–93. [7]

Smith, V. 1990, 'Split Affinities: The Case of Interracial Rape', in *Conflicts in Feminism*, eds M. Hirsch and E. F. Keller, New York, Routledge, 271–89. [1]

Snitow, A., Stansell, C. and Thompson, S. (eds) 1983, *Powers of Desire: The Politics of Sexuality*, New York, Monthly Review Press. [4]

Sontag, S. 1989, *AIDS and Its Metaphors*, New York, Farrar Strauss. [6]

Stacey, J. and Thorne, B. 1985, 'The missing feminist revolution in sociology', *Social Problems*, 32(4), 301–16. [1]

Stein, E. (ed.) 1990, *Forms of Desire: Sexual Orientation and the Social Constructionist Controversy*, New York, Garland. [5]

Stoller, R. J. 1968, *Sex and Gender*, London, Hogarth Press. [4]

Sullivan, B. 1991, 'The business of sex: Australian Government and the sex industry', *Australian and New Zealand Journal of Sociology*, 27(1), 3–18. [1]

Sullivan, B. (forthcoming), 'Film censorship: sexual politics and political culture', *Melbourne Journal of Politics*. [1]

Summers, A. 1975, *Dammed Whores and God's Police*, Ringwood, Vic., Penguin. [1]

References

Taylor, B. 1982, *Eve and the New Jerusalem: Feminism and Socialism in the Nineteenth Century*, London, Virago. [1]

Thompson, D. 1985, *Flaws in the Social Fabric: Homosexuals and Society in Sydney*, Sydney, Allen and Unwin. [5]

Thompson, D. 1989, ' "The sex/gender" distinction: a reconsideration', *Australian Feminist Studies*, 10, Summer, 23–32. [4]

Toeller, B. 1991, 'AIDS and heterosexual anal intercourse', *Archives of Sexual Behaviour*, 20(3), 233–76. [1]

Treichler, P. A. 1988a, 'AIDS, Homophobia, and Biomedical Discourse, An Epidemic of Signification', in *AIDS: Cultural Analysis, Cultural Activism*, ed. D. Crimp, Cambridge, Mass., MIT Press, 31–70. [Introd., 3]

Treichler, P. A. 1988b, 'AIDS, Gender and Biomedical Discourse', in *AIDS: The Burdens of History*, eds E. Fee and D. Fox, Berkeley, University of California Press, 190–266. [2]

Trlin, A. D., Krishnamoorthy, S. and Khoo, S.-E. 1983, 'Pre-marital sex: differentials and predictors for never-married males and females', *Australian Journal of Sex, Marriage and Family*, 4(4), 201–14. [7]

Trumbach, R. 1989a, 'The Birth of the Queen: Sodomy and the Emergence of Gender Equality in Modern Culture, 1660–1750', in *Hidden from History: Reclaiming the Gay and Lesbian Past*, eds M. B. Duberman, M. Vicinus and G. Chauncey Jr, New York, New American Library, 129–40. [5]

Trumbach, R. 1989b, 'Gender and the Homosexual Role in Modern Western Culture: The 18th and 19th Centuries Compared', in *Homosexuality, Which Homosexuality? International Conference on Gay and Lesbian Studies*, D. Altman et al., London, GMP and Amsterdam, Uitgeverij An Dekker/Schorer, 149–69. [5]

Turner, B. S. 1984, *The Body and Society*, Oxford, Blackwell. [3]

Turner, C. 1989, 'Research on sexual behaviors that transmit HIV', *AIDS*, 3 (supplement 1), 563–9. [2]

Vadasz, D. and Lipp, J. 1990, *Feeling Our Way*, Melbourne, Designer Publications. [2]

Valverde, M. 1987, *Sex, Power and Pleasure*, Philadelphia, New Society Publications. [6]

Vance, C. S. (ed.) 1984, *Pleasure and Danger, Exploring Female Sexuality*. Boston, Routledge and Kegan Paul. [6]

Vance, C. S. 1989, 'Social Construction Theory: Problems in the History of Sexuality', in *Homosexuality, Which Homosexuality? International Conference on Gay and Lesbian Studies*, D. Altman et al., London, GMP and Amsterdam, Uitgeverij An Dekker/Schorer, 13–34. [3, 4, 5]

References

Wakeling, A. 1979, 'A General Psychiatric Approach to Sexual Deviation', in *Sexual Deviation*, ed. I. Rosen, Oxford, Oxford University Press, 2nd edn, 1–28. [3]

Walkowitz, J. R. 1980, *Prostitution and Victorian Society: women, class, and the state*, Cambridge, Cambridge University Press. [3, 6]

Ward, E. 1984, *Father–Daughter Rape*, London, The Women's Press. [1]

Ward, R. 1958, *The Australian Legend*, Melbourne, Oxford University Press. [1]

Watchirs, H. 1991, *Discussion Paper: Legal Issues Relating to HIV/AIDS, Sex Workers and their Clients*, Canberra, Department of Health, Housing and Community Services. [2]

Watney, S. 1988, 'The Spectacle of AIDS', in *AIDS: Cultural Analysis, Cultural Activism*, ed. D. Crimp, Cambridge, Mass., MIT Press, 71–86. [3]

Watney, S. 1990, 'Safer Sex as Community Practice', in *AIDS: Individual, Cultural and Policy Dimensions*, eds P. Aggleton, P. Davies and G. Hart, London, Falmer Press, 19–33. [2]

Webster's Third New International Dictionary 1966, Springfield, Mass., G. and C. Merriam, unabridged. [1]

Weedon, C. 1987, *Feminist Practice and Poststructuralist Theory*, Oxford, Blackwell. [3]

Weeks, J. 1977, *Coming Out: Homosexual Politics in Britain, from the 19th Century to the Present*, London, Quartet. [3]

Weeks, J. 1981a, 'Discourse, Desire and Sexual Deviance: Some Problems in a History of Homosexuality', in *The Making of the Modern Homosexual*, ed. K. Plummer, London, Hutchinson, 76–111. [1]

Weeks, J. 1981b, *Sex, Politics and Society: The Regulation of Sexuality since 1800*, London, Longman. [1, 5]

Weeks, J. 1985, *Sexuality and its Discontents: Meanings, myths and modern sexualities*, London, Routledge and Kegan Paul. [1, 3, 4, 7]

Weeks, J. 1986, *Sexuality*, London, Horwood and Tavistock. [3]

Weeks, J. 1990, 'Sexuality and History Revisited', in *State, Private Life and Political Change*, eds L. Jamieson and H. Corr, London, Macmillan, 31–49. [5]

Weeks, J. 1991, 'Pretended Family Relationships', in *Marriage, Domestic Life and Social Change: Writings for Jacqueline Burgoyne (1944–88)*, ed. D. Clark, London, Routledge, 214–34. [5]

Weinberg, G. 1972, *Society and the Healthy Homosexual*, New York, St Martin's Press. [2]

West Australian, 26 August 1925. [6]

References

Whitam, F. and Mathy, R. 1985, *Male Homosexuality in Four Societies*, New York, Praeger. [2]

Wieringa, S. 1989, 'An Anthropological Critique of Constructionism: Berdaches and Butches', in *Homosexuality, Which Homosexuality? International Conference on Gay and Lesbian Studies*, D. Altman et al., London, GMP and Amsterdam, Uitgeverij An Dekker/Schorer, 215–38. [3]

Williams, W. 1986, *The Spirit and the Flesh: Sexual Diversity in American Indian Culture*, Boston, Beacon Press. [3]

Willis, E. 1984, 'Radical Feminism and Feminist Radicalism', in *The 60s Without Apology*, ed. S. Sayres, Minneapolis, University of Minnesota Press/Social Text, 91–118. [4]

Willis, E. 1989, The Social Relations of Medical Technology: Condoms in the AIDS Era. Paper to The Australian Sociological Association Conference, La Trobe University. [2]

Wilson, E. 1987, *Adorned in Dreams: Fashion and modernity*, Berkeley, Calif., University of California Press. [3]

Wilson, P. R. 1979, *Intimacy*, Sydney, Cassell. [7]

Wolchik, S. A., Spencer, S. L. and Lisi, I. S. 1983, 'Volunteer bias in research employing vaginal measures of sexual arousal', *Archives of Sexual Behavior*, 12(5), 339–408. [7]

Wolf, N. 1990, *The Beauty Myth*, London, Chatto and Windus. [1]

Woodhull, W. 1988, 'Sexuality, Power and the Question of Rape', in *Feminism and Foucault*, eds I. Diamond and L. Quinby, Boston, Northeastern University Press, 162–76. [1]

Woolf, V. 1977 [1928], *Orlando, A Biography*, London, Granada. [6]

Wotherspoon, G. 1991, *City of the Plain: History of a Gay Sub-Culture*, Sydney, Hale and Iremonger. [5]

Wyatt, G. E., Peters, S. D. and Guthrie, D. 1988, 'Kinsey revisited, part 1: comparisons of the sexual socialization and sexual behavior of white women over 33 years', *Archives of Sexual Behavior*, 17(3), 201–39. [7]

Yeatman, A. 1989, 'A Feminist Theory of Social Differentiation', in *Feminism/Postmodernism*, ed. L. J. Nicholson, New York, Routledge, Chapman and Hall, 281–99. [1]

Zelnik, M. and Katner, J. F. 1977, 'Sexual and contraceptive experience of young married women in the U.S.', *Family Planning Perspectives*, 6(3), 136–41. [7]

Zelnik, M. and Katner, J. F. 1980, 'Sexual activity, contraceptive use and pregnancy among metropolitan-area teenagers: 1971–1979', *Family Planning Perspectives*, 12(5), 230–7. [7]

Zimmerman, B. 1991, 'Seeing, Reading, Knowing: The Lesbian

References

Appropriation of Literature', in *(En)gendering Knowledge: Feminists in Academe*, eds J. E. Hartman and E. Messer-Davidow, Knoxville, The University of Tennessee Press, 85–99. [1]

Zinner, S. H. 1985, *STDs: Sexually Transmissible Diseases*, New York, Summit Books. [1]

INDEX

A. Parkes Electronic Mercury in Silicon Strain Gauge 15
Aborigines 17, 24
  decline in birth rate 118
abortion 9, 13, 27, 30, 78, 103, 109, 118, 138
abuse, sexual 28
  children 103, 137
acquired immune deficiency syndrome *see* AIDS
ACT UP 47
adolescents 40, 114, 135
  AIDS 137–8
  male 78
  sex education 129
  sexuality 35, 128, 137–8
  see also youth
adultery 105
advertising 33, 98
Advertising Standards Council 33
African National Congress, AIDS policy 38
Agape 123
age 73, 141
age of consent 12
aged 114
agencies, collective 72

AIDS 5, 6, 7, 9, 20, 32–48, 63, 68, 69, 71, 83, 98, 101, 102, 111, 121, 122, 136, 140
  adolescents 137–8
  educational programs 34, 35, 38–40, 42, 102, 112–16, 136
  impact of 111–16
AIDS Council of New South Wales 39
AIDS councils
  educational programs 114
  funding 43, 102
AIDS Policy Discussion Paper (1988) 114–15
Allen, J. A. 106
  Do We Need a Feminist Theory of 'the State' 103–4
  Sex and Secrets 88–9
Altman, D. 111
anal intercourse 10, 32, 54, 112
analysis
  structural 72
  log-linear 143
androgynes 65
androgyny 91, 100
Anglo-Celts 24
anorexia nervosa 17
antagonism, sexual 26

Index

anthropologists 10, 38, 107
anthropology 68–9
  ahistorical 66
anthropometrics 52
anti-discrimination legislation 111
anti-essentialism 63, 87, 97, 101
anti-humanism 14, 17
anti-war movement 78
antibiotics 111
anticlericalism 51
Aquinas, Saint Thomas 108
Archibald, J. F. 26
Archives of Sexual Behaviour 11, 14
arousal, sexual 10, 73
asceticism 51
attitudes 134–8
  measures 136
Augustine, Saint 50, 55
Australia, sexuality research 24–30, 136–43
Australian and New Zealand Journal of Sociology 97
Australian Federation of AIDS Organisations 113
Australian HIV Surveillance Reports 71
Australian Imperial Force 27
Australian IV League 113
Australian Labor Party 102, 110, 112–13
Australian National University 110

Ballard, J. A. 107
Bachofen, Ludwig 79
Bangkok 37
Bardwick, J. 90
bars 20
bath houses 20
Battersby, C.
  Gender and Genius 92, 100
battery 28
Beam, Louise *see* Dickinson, Robert

Beauvoir, Simone de *see* de Beauvoir, Simone
behaviour
  homoerotic 38
  identity and 33–8
  sexual 33–8, 139
bestiality 10, 108
'Big Business' (movie) 45
bigotry 44
bio-medicine 85
biological determinism 13
birth control 13, 78
  see also contraception
bisexuality 32, 71–2, 83, 91, 112, 134, 135
  married men 114
Black Bottom (dance) 119
black organizations 35
Blackstone's codification of laws 108
Blewett, Neal 102, 113
blood donations 83
blood transfusions 102
body practices 73
Bond, James 47
Booth, Angela 118
Braidotti, R. 100, 101
Brazil 69
Briggs, State Senator 43
Britain *see* United Kingdom
brothel-keepers 101
brothels 32
Brown, Bryan 26
Brown, N. O. 78
Bryant, Anita 43, 115
buggery 108
Bulletin, The 26
Bunny Hug (dance) 119
Burgess–Maclean case 109
Butler, J. 83, 87
Buttrose, Ita 32

California 43
Call to Australia Party 115

Index

Canada 24, 29–30, 104
  see also North America
cancer, cervical 126
capitalism 58, 60, 80, 97, 108
  monopoly 78
case histories 133
Castle, Irene & Vernon
  Modern Dancing 120
castration 93, 94
casual sex 32
CATI *see* Computer Assisted Telephone Interviewing
Catholic Church, condoms and 47
celibacy 36, 42, 47, 75
cervical cancer 126
chastity 50
  male 119
child care 103
childbirth 121
  incest and 137
children 66
  abuse 137
  masturbation 60, 86
  molesters 56, 101
  sexuality 52, 135, 137
Chile 38
China 38
chlamydia 27
Christianity 50–2
Church 104, 106
  see also Catholic Church; Church of England; Devil; God; Methodist Church; religion
Church of England 109
cinema 96
  see also movies
circumcision, female 87
civil liberties 75, 78
Cixous, H. 94
class
  middle 133
  oppression 79

permissiveness 135
sexuality 61–2
working 78, 79, 87, 104
clitoridectomy 87
clones 65, 82
clubs 37
Cockburn, C. 98
Code Napoleon 108
coitus 108
  measuring 10
Collins, J. K. & Robinson, L. 138
  see also McCabe, M. P.
comedy 26
Committee on Homosexual Offences and Prostitution (Great Britain) 109
Commonwealth AIDS Research Grants Committee 45
compulsory heterosexuality 65, 127, 128–9
Computer Assisted Telephone Interviewing (CATI) 142
condoms 39, 40, 41, 42, 45, 47, 114, 118
conduct, sexual 85–6, 97
conferences 24
  HIV/AIDS (Hobart, 1988) 113
conjugation 59
Connell, Robert 70, 96, 105–6
consent 109–10
  age of 12
Consumer Health Forum 113
contraception 9, 10, 13, 72, 103, 118, 134, 135, 137
  see also Pill
control systems 61
  see also power; State
convicts 24, 118
coprophilia 10
core gender identity 89
counselling services
  psychiatric 139
  sexual 139
Coxon, T. 139

170

Index

Crawford, J. 40
Criminal Law Amendment Act 1885 (Great Britain) 108
Criminal Offences Act (Great Britain) 110
criminologists 9
cultural theorists 6, 10
culture, biological foundations of 59
cunnilingus 54

Daly, M. 95
dancing 119–20, 124
  see also specific dances
Darwin, C. 49, 52
  Descent of Man 52
Darwinists, social 13
Davies, P. 140
Davis, Catherine
  Factors in the Sex Life of 22,000 Women 132
Davis, Ken 123
de Beauvoir, Simone 95, 101
de Lauretis, T. 96–7
de Sade, Marquis 56
decadence, Western 38
Decameron 51
deconstructionist framing theory 62–4
decriminalization of homosexual behaviour 43, 108–11
defence forces 115
degeneracy, sexual 52
D'Emilio, J. *see* Freedman, E. B.
deployment of sexuality 61
desirability, sexual 73
determinism, biological 13
detumescence 59
deviance, sexual 62, 65, 74, 86, 104, 114
Devil 51
diaries 74, 139, 140, 141
Dickinson, Robert & Beam, Louise
  One Thousand Marriages 132
difference, sexual 94–5
dimorphism, sexual 13
Dinnerstein, D. 57, 70
discourse theory 62, 70, 84–9, 96, 106
discrimination 43, 111, 115
  see also anti-discrimination
diseases
  sexually transmitted 27, 102, 112, 122, 138, 139, 140, 143
  see also AIDS; cervical cancer; gonorrhoea; HIV; syphilis; venereal diseases
diversity, sexual 20
divorce 12, 13, 27, 103, 109
Don Juan 51
drag queens 65
drugs
  sulpha 117
  users 37, 84, 112
drunkenness 30
DuBois, E. 122
Duncan, George 43
dykes 65
  see also lesbianism
dysfunction, sexual 137

'E Street' (television program) 45
Economic and Social Research Council
  'Issues in Researching Sexual Behaviour' 140
educational programs 35, 38–40, 42, 102, 112–16, 136
  schools 39
effeminacy 82
Ellis, B. J. 13
Ellis, Havelock 38, 52, 53, 58, 77, 131, 132
emotion 92
emotional attachment 70
Engels, Friedrich 79
epidemics *see* AIDS; HIV

Index

epidemiologists 9
epistemologies 88
equality 75, 84, 119
Eros 64, 123
erotic role-playing 10
erotic unresponsiveness 10
eroticism 72
eroticization 11–12, 41
essentialism 14, 50, 63, 87–8, 94, 97, 100
   see also anti-essentialism
ethnicity 107, 141
ethnography 58, 68
eugenicists 13
Europe 69, 108
Evans, A. *see* Hansen, C. E.
evolution 13
exotica 58
exploitation, of women 81

face-to-face interviews 142
family 57, 80, 103
   breakdown 139
   planning 109
   size 27, 137
fantasies 15, 36, 41, 73, 98, 99, 125
fashion 73
'Fast Forward' (television program) 26
fear 126, 128
fellatio 54
female circumcision 87
female specificity 77, 101
femaleness 92, 95
feminism 64, 65
   sex definitions 88
   sexuality and 16–18, 40
feminity, males and 100
fertility 73, 138
   see also in vitro fertilization
fetishes 55
fidelity 40
Field, J. & Wadsworth, J. 140

film and media theorists 10
films *see* movies
First Fleet 118
fitness 73
Flexner, Eleanor 122
football, homoerotic behaviour and 38
foreplay 54, 81
Foucault, M. 38, 52, 59–60, 61, 62, 73, 74, 84, 86, 87, 88, 96, 104, 107, 108, 113, 120
frame theories of sexuality 49–75
frameworks of sexuality 5–31, 56–64, 86, 90
France 63, 90, 94, 108
free love 13
Freedman, E. B. & D'Emilio, J. 104
French Revolution 108
Freud, S. 12, 13, 38, 49, 52–3, 54, 55, 57, 66, 74, 78, 81, 85, 90, 93, 94, 125, 131, 132, 133
   Civilization and its Discontents 64
   Three Essays on Sexuality 97
frontier theses 29–30
funding
   AIDS councils 43, 102
   HIV/AIDS programs 114, 115
   research 17, 46, 53

Gagnon, J. H. 40, 131, 132, 133
   & Simon, W. 54, 56, 59, 61, 85
   Sexual Conduct 85, 86
Gallipoli 27
Gatens, M. 100
Gay and Lesbian Mardi Gras (Sydney) 47
gay communities 34, 36
   identifying 36
gay liberation 19, 62, 64, 72, 74, 75
gay machismo 89
Gay Men's Community Health Centre 48

Index

gay plague 33
gay rights 111
gay-bashing 44
  see also poofter-bashing
gays *see* gay communities;
  homosexuality
gender 66–73
  definition 88, 96
  differentiation 11
  freaks 82
  genius and 92
  identity and 93–4
  orders 95
  perspectives 89–93
  physical 90
  politics 79 *see also* power
  psychological 90
  regimes 95
  sexuality and 76–101
  social structure and 95–7
genital herpes 27, 126
genital warts 27, 126
genito-physiology 11
genius, gender and 92
German Empire, homosexuality in 108
gerontologists 9, 10
Gestalt 59, 68
Glassner, B. 73
Global Programme on AIDS (GPA) 34, 141
God 34
Goldman, R. J. & Goldman, J. 137
gonorrhoea 117, 118, 119, 126
governments, gay organizations and 48
  see also State
GPA *see* Global Programme on AIDS
Greece, Ancient 107
Greenwich Village 120
Gregory VIII, Pope 50
Grim Reaper 114

Grizzly Bear (dance) 119
Guteck, B. A. 99
gynaecologists 9

Hall, S. 109–10
Hamilton, George
  A Study in Marriage 132
Hansen, C. E. & Evans, A. 134
harassment, sexual 9, 28, 67, 103
Hawke Labor government 112–13
Hayden, Bill 110
Hearn, J. & Parkin, W. 67, 95, 98
hegemonies 61–2, 107, 132
Helms Amendment (USA) 115
hemaphrodism 97
Hendrick, S. & Hendrick, C. 134
Henry VIII, King 108
Henslin, J. M. 135
Herdt, G. 68–9
herpes, genital 27, 126
heterosexism 21–2, 43–4
heterosexual community, definition of 36–7
heterosexuality 21–3, 57, 81
  compulsory 65, 127, 128–9
  institutionalized 95
  males 114
  monogamous 33
  women 75
Hispanics 35
historians 6, 10, 95
history of sexuality 5
Hite, Shere 20, 25
HIV 5, 6, 7, 9, 20, 27, 32–48, 50, 51, 63, 68, 71–2, 75, 83, 98, 101, 102, 111, 121, 122, 126, 140, 141
  adolescents 137–8
  anti-bodies 41
  compared to syphilis 122
  educational programs 33–4, 102, 136
  health promotion 69, 112–16

173

Index

heterosexual transmission 103
impact 111–16
HIV/AIDS Conference (Hobart, 1988) 113
Hogan, Paul 26
Hollway, W. 96
'Home and Away' (television program) 45
homoerotic behaviour 38
homophobia 23, 43–4
homosexuality 9, 19–20, 32–48, 60–1, 71, 75, 76, 77, 81–2, 91, 135, 136, 138
  Australian Labor Party and 102, 110, 112–13
  cross-cultural expression 37
  decriminalization 43, 108–11
  deviance 62, 104
  legislation 32, 115–16
  lesbianism *see* lesbianism
  male 10, 13, 19, 27, 71, 82, 86, 108–9
  masculinity and 74
  Masters and Johnson 53–4
  minority practice 69
  models 37–8
  persecution 38
  rape 28
  regulation 107–11
  rights 63
  sex and identity 38–42
  State and 105–16
  term coined 61
  see also gay liberation
Hong, S.-M. 136–7
housewives 71
human immunodeficiency virus (HIV) *see* HIV
Humanist Society 110
humour, asceticism and 51
hysterical women 60, 86

identity
  behaviour and 33–8

core gender 89
  gender and 93–4
  sexual 33–8, 82, 136
illegitimacy 13
imagination 92
immigration 115
immunologists 9
impotency 10, 36
in vitro fertilization 73
incest 10, 17
  effect on childbirth 137
incommensurabilities 14–24, 31
individualism 71
infidelity 27
information, sexual 131–43
institutes, sexuality research 11
inter-generational sex 28–9
interactionism, symbolic 85
intercourse 53, 54
  anal 10, 32, 54, 112
  see also coitus
interdisciplinary fields of research 6–31
Intergovernmental Committee on AIDS 115
interviews 141
  face-to-face 142
  telephone 140, 141
intuition 92
Iran 38
Irigaray, L. 94, 95
Irish people 25

Jack-Off parties 42, 48
Johnson, V. E. *see* Masters, W. H.
Joint Centre for Survey Methods Newsletter 140
Journal of Sex Research 11
journals 11, 24, 35
Jung, Carl G. 92
Jungian psychology 92

KAPB studies 34
Keat, R. 73

Index

Kent, S. K.
Sex and Suffrage in Britain 1860–1914 122
Kinsey, A. C. 25, 26, 53, 54, 67, 77, 78, 79, 97, 98, 133–5, 139
  methodology 133–4
kinship 59, 66, 105
Kinsman, G. 104
Kippax, S. 40
kiss-in 47
Klein, F. 134
Koedt, A.
Myth of Vaginal Orgasm 81
Krafft-Ebing, R. von 131
Psychopathia Sexualis 52
Kristeva, J. 67–8, 83
Kuhn, T. S. 54

Lacan, Jacques 83, 84, 94
Lakatos, I. 54
language 67–8, 70, 73, 90
Lauretis, T. de *see* de Lauretis, T.
Legal Working Group of the Australian Federation of AIDS Organisations 115
legislation
  anti-discrimination 111
  homosexuality 32, 115–16
Leidholt, D. & Raymond, J. G. 126
lesbian continuum 65
lesbianism 10, 12, 13, 17, 19, 27, 44, 47, 56, 63, 81, 83–4, 97, 109, 123, 125
Lévi-Strauss, Claude 66
Leviticus 108
liberalism, sexual 13
liberation
  gay 19, 62, 64, 72, 74, 75
  sexual 6, 74
libertarianism 13, 123, 124
  urban 26
libertinage 56
libido 55, 77, 94

Libya 38
linguistics *see* language
Lisrel 142
literary critics 10
Local Government Act 1988 (Great Britain)
  Clause 28 115–16
log-linear analysis 143
lust 50
Luther, Martin 51

McCabe, M. P. & Collins, J. K. 137
McIntyre, Martha 38
MacKinnon, C. A. 88, 98
  Towards a Feminist Theory of the State 103
Macquarie University 39
McQueen D. 140
males, homosexual *see* homosexuality, male
Malinowski, B. 68
  Sex and Repression in Savage Society 58
  The Sexual Life of Savages 58
Malthusian couple 60, 86
Marbury, Bessie 120, 124
Marcuse, H. 13, 58, 61, 78, 79, 80, 87
marriage 12, 13, 72, 78, 103, 105, 107, 109
  see also divorce
Marshall, J. 82
Marx, Karl 78, 81
Marxism 13, 17, 65, 84
masculinity
  Australian 25
  heterosexual 101
  homosexuality and 74
  women and 91, 100
mass media 35, 98, 102
massage 41
Masters, W. H. & Johnson, V. E. 53–4, 59, 77

Index

homosexuality and 53–4
Human Sexual Response 78
masturbation 10, 41, 42, 54, 108
   children 60, 86
maternity 17
Matthews, J. 95
Mead, M. 68
Medicare 113
Merson, Mike 34
Methodist Church 119
methodology, sexual research 139, 140
middle class 133
   women 87
Middle East 37
Millet, K. 64, 81
   Sexual Politics 89
Minow, M. 107
misogyny 23, 25
'Mr Bubbles' 56
Mitchell, J. 66, 83, 93
   Woman's Estate 65
modernism 77–84
monasticism 50
monogamy 34–5, 40, 41–2, 45, 47
   serial 27, 35
monopoly capitalism 78
Montagu–Wildeblood trial 109
moralism 123
Mort, F. 110
movie houses 37
movies 15, 45
Mozart, W. 52
multi-dimensional attitude measures 136
multiculturalism 47
music 51

National Academy of Sciences 46
National AIDS Education Campaign
   Benchmark Survey 136
National Health and Medical Research Council 45

National HIV/AIDS Strategy 115
national specificity 24–30
nativism 50–6, 71, 72, 74
   scientific 52
natural selection 52
necrophilia 10
'Neighbours' (television program) 45
New Left 78, 79, 80, 81
New South Wales 111
   declining birth-rate 118
   decriminalization of homosexual behaviour 43
New South Wales Anti-Discrimination Board 111
New York 42
New Zealand 24, 39, 110, 118
Nile, Fred 46–7, 115
non-marital sexuality 17
normality 62
North America 69
   see also Canada; United States of America

object choice 54
obligation 126–9
obscenity 26
obstetricians 9
occupations, sex and 135
ockers 25
Oedipal attachments 90, 93
old age 10
Old Left 78
oppression
   class 79
   structural 65
   women 19–20, 64, 65, 80
oral sex 10, 98
organization sexuality 67
orgasms 10, 42, 78, 81, 125, 134
Orton, S. & Quick, S. 140
the Other, theory of 95

paediatricians 9

Index

paedophiles 71, 135
paedophilia 9, 10, 17, 20
Pankhurst, Christabel 129
  The Great Scourge and How To End It 118–19
Papua-New Guinea 69
Paris 42, 120
Parkin, W. *see* Hearn, J.
parochialism 25, 29
partners, sexual 41
Pateman, C. 88, 89, 105
'Patient Zero' 52
patriarchy 80, 93, 103, 105
  see also State
pay-TV, pornography and 28
peer pressure 128
pelvic inflammatory disease 126
penicillin 27, 117, 122
penile penetration 12
penile tumescence 14–15, 19
permissiveness 74, 78, 109, 134, 138
  class and 135
persecution 38, 110, 111
personality traits 90, 91
perversions 56, 104
phallocentricity 94
philosophers 10
physical gender 90
Piercy, Marge
  The Grand Coolie Damn 81
Pill 26, 78, 111
pimps 101
play, homosexual behaviour and 38
pleasure 13, 98, 125–6, 128
  women's 13
Plummer, K.
  Sexual Stigma 85, 86
police 28
political movements 27
political theorists 6, 10
politics
  feminist 95

gender 79
of research 97–101
sexual 11–14, 64, 81, 117–30, 138
  see also power
Pollack, M. 62
polymorphous perverse, theory of 79, 80
poofter-bashing 43, 44
popular culture 26, 71
population 104, 106
pornography 13, 17, 20, 28, 41, 88, 98, 99, 103, 105
post-modernism 14, 17
post-structuralism 84–5, 101
power, sexuality and 11–12, 61–2, 64, 70, 74, 75, 80–1, 86, 87, 88, 89, 91, 93, 95, 98
pre-marital sexuality 12, 134, 135, 137
pre-marital virginity 137
preferences, sexual 134
pregnancy 126, 139
  juvenile 128
premature ejaculations 10
'Pretty Woman' (movie) 45
preventative campaigns 33, 69, 112
priapism 10
priests 51
primitivism 58
Pringle, R. 67
prisoners 59
prisons 28, 48, 56
procreation, sexuality and 58
productivity 104
promiscuity 13, 34, 46, 80, 118
prophylactics *see* condoms
prosecution 109
prostitutes 59, 71, 105, 109, 112
prostitution 9, 13, 17, 20, 28, 32, 33, 35, 37, 46, 103, 104, 105, 108, 109, 115
Prussia 108

psychiatric counselling 139
psychiatrists 6, 9
psychiatry, forensic 71
psychoanalysis 45, 57, 58, 64, 66, 78, 83, 94, 133
psychoanalytic sociology 57
psychological gender 90
psychologists 6, 90, 91
psychology 53, 57, 106
   Jungian 92
psychometrics 134
Public Health Association 113
public sex 20

Queensland 32, 102, 110, 113
questionnaires 132, 141

race 135
random sampling techniques 134, 136
rape 9, 17, 28, 30, 48, 56, 105
   homosexual 28
rapists 101
red plague 27
redemptive reinvention of sex 123
regression 142–3
Reich, W. 13, 57, 73, 80, 81
Reiche, R. 78
relational self 94
religion 56, 105
   see also Catholic Church; Church; Church of England; Christianity; Devil; God; Methodist Church
religiosity, adolescents and 137–8
religious scholars 10
repression 60, 87, 100, 104, 120
repressive desublimation 79
reproduction 81, 107
   obligatory 127
   technology 138
research 131–43
   Australian 136–43

   comparative 29
   education 44–6
   feminist 16–18, 22
   frameworks 5–31
   funding 17, 25, 46, 53
   HIV/AIDS 34
   homosexuality 19–21, 23
   incommensurabilities 14–24, 31
   institutes of 11
   instruments 141
   interdisciplinary fields 6–31
   methodology 19, 73, 136–7, 139, 140
   national context 7
   national specificity 24–30
   overseas 39
   politics 11–14, 16, 87–101
   prevention emphasis 44–6
   publications 11
   rationales 7
   sexological 139
   socio-behavioural 29
   transnational 29
   volunteers 134
rest and recreation 105
Rich, A. 95
Rio de Janeiro 37
risk behaviour 41, 112
risk groups 41, 71–2, 101, 112, 113
Robinson, L. see Collins, J. K.
role theory 72, 90, 91
role-playing, erotic 10
Rout, Ettie 118
Royal Commission on the Decline in the Birth-Rate and on the Mortality of Infants in New South Wales (1904) 118
Royal Commission on Venereal Diseases 1910 (Great Britain) 117
Rubin, G. 82, 98
rural communities 114

Index

Sade, Marquis de *see* de Sade, Marquis
sado-masochism 20, 82, 135
sado-masochistic strips 41
safe sex 34, 40, 41, 47, 72, 75, 98, 101, 128
sampling techniques, random 134, 136
San Francisco 42
SAPA *see* Social Aspects of Prevention of AIDS (SAPA)
saunas, homosexual 32, 37, 42
Scarlet Alliance 113
Schaffer, K. 107
Schiavi, R. C. 134
schools
   HIV/AIDS education in 38
   homosexuality and 105
science, sexuality and 50–6
scripts
   sexual 86
   social 56–7, 59–60
secretaries 67, 98–9
self, relational 94
self regulation 111
self-images 73
semiotics 68, 72
serial monogamy 27, 35
sex
   aids 10
   appetites 59
   definition 88
   drives 55
      see also libido
   education 13, 106, 129
      see also educational programs
   imbalance 25
   industry 28
   intergenerational 28
   research *see* research
   roles 90, 91
   safe 34, 40, 41, 47, 72, 75, 98, 101, 128
   workers 6, 34, 102

sexological research 139
sexologists 6, 9, 124
sexology 13, 52, 54, 61, 85, 125
sexual abuse 28
   children 103
sexual activity 134–8
   first 27
sexual arousal 10, 73
sexual behaviour 33–8, 139
sexual communities 6
sexual conduct 85–6, 97
sexual counselling 139
sexual degeneracy 52
sexual desirability 73
sexual difference 94–5
sexual dimorphism 13
sexual diversity 20
sexual dysfunction 137
sexual harassment 9, 28, 67, 103
sexual identities 33–8, 82, 136
sexual liberalism 13
sexual liberation 6, 74
   equality and 75
Sexual Offences Act (Great Britain) 109
sexual outlets 135
sexual partners, numbers of 41
sexual politics 11–14, 64, 81, 117–30, 138
   see also feminism; power
sexual practices 41
   see also homosexuality
sexual preferences, measurement of 134
sexual scripts 86
sexual selection 52
sexual stimulus 10
sexual subcultures 6
sexual variation 10
sexuality
   Australian study 139–43
   categories 71, 106
   children 52

Index

class and 61–2, 78, 79, 87, 104, 114
definitions 8, 22–3, 35, 98, 124–5
deployment of 61
deviance 62, 65, 74, 86, 104, 114
female 77
frame theories 49–75
gender and 76–101
history 5
information on 131–43
non-marital 12
organization 67
power and 11–12, 61–2, 64, 70, 117–30
pre-marital 12, 134, 135, 137
procreation and 58
race and 135
regulation 105
representation in the arts 54–5
see also movies; television; videos
reproductive 107
research *see* research
science and 50–6
social structure and 135
self-regulation 111
semiotics 68, 72
social structure 64–75
State and 102–16
Western 12, 13–14
workplace 67
sexualization 11–12
sexually transmitted diseases 27, 102, 112, 122, 138, 139, 140, 143
see also AIDS; gonorrhoea; HIV; syphilis; venereal diseases
Shorter, Edward 117
Showalter, Elaine
Sexual Anarchy 122
Simon, W. *see* Gagnon, J. H.

Sinclair, Ian 102
single parents 103
households 27
Social Aspects of Prevention of AIDS (SAPA) 39, 40, 42, 46
social Darwinists 13
social relations 66–8
social scripts 56–7, 59–60
social structure, gender and 95–7
sexuality and 135
socialism 13
sociologists 6, 10, 90, 95
sociology, psychoanalytic 57
sodomy 32, 108
Sontag, Susan
AIDS and Its Metaphors 122
South Africa 38
South Australia 43, 110, 111
South-east Asia 69
specificity 81, 104
female 77, 101
national 24–30
sports, homosexuality and 105
State 62, 71, 102–16
policies 106
welfare 106
sterilization 13
stimulus, sexual 10
Stoller, R. J. 89
stripping, sado-masochistic 41
structural analysis 72
structure in sexuality 64–75
student movement 78
studies
Australian 139–43
subcultures, sexual 6
sulpha drugs 117
surplus repression 79
surplus value 79
surveys 39, 138
Australian 140–3
symbolic interactionism 85
symbolism 67, 68, 70
Sydney 120

180

Index

Sydney Hospital for Sick Children 118
syphilis 111, 117, 118, 126
   compared to HIV 122

taboos 38
tales, bawdy 51
Tasmania 33, 110, 113
technologies of gender 96
technology of sex 96
telephone interviews 140, 141
television 45
Third World 17, 37
Thompson, D. 88
Thompson, Jack 26
tolerance 32–3
tomboys 100
transexuality 20, 56, 71, 89
transsexuals 71
transvestism 20
Trobriand Islanders 58
tumescence 125
   penile 14–15, 19
Turkey Trot (dance) 119
Turner, B. S. 73

United Kingdom 24, 40, 104, 108–10, 111, 113, 115, 117–18, 122
United Nations 28
United States of America 24, 25, 29–30, 33, 35, 94, 104, 111, 113, 115, 122, 132, 133, 135, 138–9
   see also North America
universalization 100–1
unresponsiveness, erotic 10
urban libertarianism 26
urolangia 10
urologists 9

vaginismus 10
Valverde, M. 126
Vance, C. S. 62, 63, 87, 126

variation, sexual 10
venereal diseases 9, 27, 117–19
   rates of infection 117, 121
venereology 34
   see also venereal diseases
Victoria 137
Victorian AIDS Council 33, 48
videos, pornographic 28
violence 27, 30, 56, 72, 103
   anti-homosexual 43
virginity 27, 36
   pre-marital 137
virility 92
volunteers, in sexuality research 134

Waldby, C. 40
Wadsworth, J. *see* Field, J.
Walkowitz, J. R. 117–18
war 25
Ward, Russel
   The Australian Legend 25
warts, genital 27, 126
Weeks, J. 62, 104, 108–9
Weir, Peter 26
welfare state 106
Western Australia 32
Western decadence 38
Western sexuality 12, 13–14
White, Patrick
   The Tree of Man 25
Whitehouse, Mary 115
Whitlam Labor government 110
WHO Global Programme on AIDS (GPA) 34, 141
Wilde, Oscar 108
Williamson, David 26
Wisconsin 43
Wolfenden, Lord 109, 116
women
   child-bearing 27
   exploitation 81
   heterosexuality and 75
   middle-class 87

Index

oppression and 19–20, 64, 65, 80
Woolf, Virginia 120–1, 123
working class 78, 79, 87, 104
workplace, sexuality and the 67, 98–9

World AIDS Day 47
World War I 118–19
wowserism 123

youth 59, 114
   see also adolescents